an EDUCATION
IN POLITICS

an EDUCATION
IN POLITICS
Four Years in the Iowa State Senate 2004-2008

DAVE MULDER
and
FRANK B. WOOD, JR.

iUniverse, Inc.
Bloomington

AN EDUCATION IN POLITICS
Four Years in the Iowa State Senate 2004-2008

iUniverse books may be ordered through booksellers or by contacting:

iUniverse
1663 Liberty Drive
Bloomington, IN 47403
www.iuniverse.com
1-800-Authors (1-800-288-4677)

ISBN: 978-1-4759-4776-2 (sc)
ISBN: 978-1-4759-4775-5 (ebk)

Library of Congress Control Number: 2012916137

Printed in the United States of America

iUniverse rev. date: 09/10/2012

Table of Contents

Forward

During my time as Governor of Iowa, I've had the great privilege to work with dedicated and talented public servants from all across the state. Dave Mulder and Frank Wood truly represent the very best of what it means to be a "citizen-legislator." During their time under Iowa's golden dome, they served with dignity, with honor, and with a real interest in bipartisanship. Most importantly, they never forgot who they were or where they came from.

So, what bonds do these two former State Senators from different parties and different regions of Iowa share? Well, it's very simple: a belief in God, life-long educators, and the strong character that has defined generations of dedicated public servants from Iowa including visionaries like Henry A. Wallace, Norman Borlaug, and Annie Wittenmeyer.

Sen. Wood has always been a champion of public education for Iowa's children. He's a tireless advocate for students, parents, and teachers. He believes we need to do all we can to prepare our young people for the very competitive 21st century economy.

Sen. Mulder is a reasoned, pragmatic public servant who made a difference by supporting legislation to reduce tobacco use, promote education, and increase access to health care for all Iowans.

Finally, we can all be very thankful Frank Wood and Dave Mulder decided to collaborate and put these inspiring words of wisdom into book form. There is no doubt that many important faith-based life lessons, as well as keen political insight, can and will be learned for generations to come because of their efforts.

Iowa State Governor Chet Culver.

For Dot, my wife of 50 years. No man has been blessed more than I with such a wonderful wife. Without her consent and motivation, I would never have considered running for office.

And I offer special thanks to Frank for his friendship and many contributions. I must also thank Jodi Grover and Peg Juffer for reading, correcting, and encouragement. Special thanks to cousin Lianne Mercer for her editing skills, ideas, and assistance in getting this book published. I also want to thank all of those Iowa Senators (both parties) for their willingness to work with me and for all they taught me. Actually that holds true for all of the great people at the Capitol. It was also a pleasure to work with Governors Vilsack and Culver. But the most of my thanks go to my Lord and Savior Jesus Christ—He knows me, yet He still loves me.

Dave Mulder

For my wife, Peggy, and for my family. Without their love, support, and understanding, I would not have been willing to even think about running for public office.

I would like to go on and thank Senator Dave Mulder for his determination and fortitude in pushing me through this process of putting my thoughts on these pages. It was my request to Dave to write this book in the first place, and if it weren't for his drive, we wouldn't have accomplished our goal. I hope that you will learn from and enjoy reading both Dave's and my personal stories about our four years in the Iowa legislature.

Frank B. Wood, Jr.

"Being a politician is a poor profession. Being a public servant is a noble one."

President Herbert Hoover

Preface

Why would two first-time, one-time legislators want to write a book about politics? Why would you want to read it? Is it all sour grapes? Nope! It's probably 90% positive, but the 10% that's negative needs to be exposed, analyzed, and corrected. This book isn't just for politicians (although it is for them, too); it's for the average person who cares about the how, what, and why of creating our laws.

Both of us are educators, love kids, and are patriotic towards our great state and country. Frank is a former Republican who turned Democrat, and Dave is a life-long Republican who worked readily with Democrats. Dave says, "We first met at the orientation session held in Des Moines in December following our election. But our friendship really began on the second day of our first session. Frank's seat in the Senate was right behind me. Both of us were, and continue to be, early arrivals. I invited him down to the cafeteria for an early breakfast, and it grew from there."

We learned that amazing things can happen when parties work together and very little good comes when they don't. Did we friends agree on every issue? Far from it. Democrats and Republicans do have definite differences and ways of getting things done. The goals may be similar or the same, but the methodology might not even be close. Party affiliation should not determine or break up friendships. Sometimes people have to agree to disagree.

One thing we agreed upon was the fact that our spouses and family played integral roles. Neither of us could have done our jobs as State Senators without their support. Being a legislator takes a lot of energy, patience, study, and time. Somewhere between 1200 and 1500 bills are introduced each session. About 300 or so of those will become law. No legislator knows a lot about everything. In fact, there was a lot more we didn't know than what we did. Being a legislator means being in a strong educational process with a high and steep learning curve. Knowing this should make one more humble and less arrogant, but that isn't always the case. You'll read of some examples. On the other hand, every legislator has his/her areas of expertise and special interest.

Finding the best and most knowledgeable legislators working on the right bills is imperative. We will discuss many issues in this book. It is not our purpose to convince you that our position was the right one. We will always let you know what we think or how we voted, but whether we were right or wrong is for you to decide.

Following the written portion of the book is an Appendix. This is intended to define and further describe certain terms or procedures for those of you who may not be as familiar with them as others are. These terms and procedures may be important—so at these times, we will ask you to go to the Appendix and find out more. When you see *, you will find a brief explanation following closely in the text.

Contact information and a brief biography of each author are in the back of the book. Feel free to contact us. We welcome your input. Both of us left office in 2008; this gives us a bit more perspective on what was accomplished while we were there, what seems to be lasting, and what has fallen by the wayside.

Check the chapter titles in the Table of Contents. What interests you? Start reading. Get involved. What do you think needs changing? How might you go about it? Who would you contact? Do you know who your legislators are?

"Politics makes strange bedfellows."

Charles Dudley Warner

CHAPTER 1

Philosophies (Right or Wrong) in Politics

DAVE

Some philosophies held by political parties make some sense but can be hard to live with. It's a common belief that it's a legislator's responsibility to pass the best bills possible. This is not adhered to by many in the minority party, and it doesn't make any difference which party is in the minority. Here are eight quotes we heard during our first year in the Legislature:

1. "Do whatever it takes to get back in the majority."
2. "Don't help the majority party by improving a bad bill." (Let them pass it and make them pay at the polls in November.)
3. "Make the majority party members take * 'bad votes'."
4. "The only power a minority party has is time and * 'papering a bill' with numerous amendments."
5. "The only decision the minority party has to make is, 'Where shall we meet for dinner tonight'?"
6. "Record everything; use selected quotes and votes against your opponent in November."
7. "Know who your friends are—and they aren't on the other side of the aisle."
8. "All is fair in love and politics."

* An example of making a legislator take a 'bad vote' would be when one would force the opposing members to vote against a popular

issue. Let's say there is a bill that already has adequate funding for the blind in it, but then an amendment for an additional million to go to the blind is added. This has to be voted down because it was a budget buster. Those who voted against it will be cast in the role of taking a "bad vote" against the blind. So when you read that someone voted against the blind, abortion, poor, or any other controversial issue, check out the circumstances and how the actual vote was taken.

    * 'Papering a bill' is a tactic used by the minority party to prolong the issue, cause 'bad votes', and sometimes just antagonize the other party. It is a costly waste of time and money but just one of a number of games politicians play.

Many of the above quotes are true. In politics, the majority party controls the agenda. The first two years we were part of a Senate that had 25 Democrats and 25 Republicans. That meant every committee had equal numbers of Rs and Ds, and there were co-chairs who set the agenda in alternate weeks.

There were also co-majority leaders and co-presidents who took control in alternate weeks. This was unique; it hadn't happened in Iowa in nearly 50 years. One positive factor was that every issue could "get on the table" and the parties "needed" each other in order to pass anything. The Governor was a Democrat so this was an advantage to that party because of his potential veto, and the power of the * 'bully pulpit.'

    * 'Bully pulpit' is the power of the highest office. In this case it is the Governor. He always has an audience and the press. Everything he says or does is recorded and given statewide publicity. His "pulpit" is bigger and better than anyone else's. The term was coined by the 26th President, Theodore Roosevelt, who recognized that the incumbent President had an opportunity like few others to share his views and exhort or inspire others to believe as he did.

The 25/25 was interesting and quite productive, but it is not the ideal. It can give too much power to an already powerful position, i.e., the governorship. It also presents problems for the other branch, in this case, the House of Representatives. While the Senate was in balance at 25/25, the House was in control of the Republicans by a slim 51 to 49 margin. A balanced branch or a slim majority present some other problems in terms of illness and absenteeism. No controversial issue will be taken to committee, or to the floor, if a member(s) is not present.

Leaders do not (maybe even will not) bring up a bill that isn't going to pass. We'll speak much more about this later.

The final two years we served saw a new Democrat as Governor, a 30-20 Democrat advantage in the Senate, and a 53-47 majority in the House. This meant that every committee was chaired by a Democrat; each committee had two Rs to every three Ds; the Senate Majority Leader was a Democrat, and so was the President of the Senate. This meant that the only time the Democrats actually needed Republicans was for a gubernatorial appointment requiring a 2/3 majority Senate vote. This would require at least 4 Republicans to vote for an appointee if all the Democrats hung together. Of course some Rs might also be needed if five or more Ds were in opposition to a bill. Also, 30-20 is not 'veto-proof'.

We'll talk more in Chapter 4 about majority power and some of the situations that develop. But this chapter is about philosophy. Think about those statements made earlier in this chapter. Are these things you want to know about when you talk to a future sitting legislator? Does this person have a servant's heart (because that's what a legislator is) or a ruler's attitude?

This is extremely important to consider. When does the philosophy of the party supersede the opinions, attitudes, or values of the legislator? Should a legislator ever vote against the wishes of his/her constituents? Our answers to these two questions are seldom and yes. Following are some anecdotal situations which we hope will help you understand the philosophies and how we feel about them.

When I campaigned for the Senate seat, I felt it important to promise to work only for the things in which I held firm convictions, and then to try keep an open mind on all the other issues. Here are the issues I selected:

Education would be my Number 1 priority with emphasis on what is good for kids.

I am pro-life.

Increase the Cigarette Tax $1 per pack. (From 36 cents to $1.36).

I would not vote to increase the amount of gambling opportunities in Iowa.

I wanted to establish legislator term limits of 12 years.

I wanted to get an additional penny for the can and bottle redemption centers.

I promised to work hard, listen, and always be available.

Remember, we are not necessarily trying to convince you we are right with the positions we supported. They are mentioned to help you understand the difficulty in establishing and maintaining a position as a legislator. Now let's examine each of these issues and see what happened behind the scenes as well as what resolution may have been achieved.

Bottle/can redemption—

Iowa passed a "bottle/can redemption law" in 1978 which requires a nickel deposit when the merchandise is purchased and is refunded when the empties are returned. At the time of passage, the redemption centers received a penny for processing and recycling the empties. I wanted these centers to receive an additional penny because they were now losing money. Costs had increased significantly in the 28 years or so, but the revenue was the same as when the bill was passed. Just think about the inflation, higher minimum wages, increased gas prices, and many other costs that had gone up in those years. During this time Iowa had gone from over 300 redemption centers across the state to fewer than 100. I had promised to author a bill to increase the amount by another penny. This cost is paid by the companies that produce the products. I did not foresee the problems that would arise as I supported this issue.

For every 100 cans and bottles that are sold, about 16 are never returned. This fact alone makes several million dollars for the various suppliers because the nickel is never paid back.

Grocery stores like HyVee and Fareway do not like to redeem the empties because of the filthy items being located near food products. I don't like that either! Major bottlers and suppliers like Pepsi, Coke, Budweiser and other distributors favor curbside recycling because of far less cost and hassle for them. Therefore, all of the above donate considerably to both parties so that the issue does not become a debate on the floor. Leaders, not liking to bring up controversial items where they do not know the voting outcome, and where they do not want to quench income resources, let sleeping dogs lie. So every year there was a lot of backroom discussing, bill writing, etc., but no action was ever passed out of committee or brought to the floor. In our last year, because we had a governor who went out on a limb in support of these redemption centers, legislation was passed (in the *Standings Bill) which provided $1M that could be applied for as grants to cover losses. It helped but was a far cry from solving the problem. Why stay in business to just break even?

* Standings Bill. This is the final bill of the session in most cases. It is described as a "Christmas Tree" because everything is attached to it. It's incredibly long and deals with every issue that couldn't find a home in a more proper place. Legislation can be hidden in there, and usually only the Governor (or some very alert staff member or lobbyist) will find it. The Governor may use his "line item veto" on this bill and often does.

As much as I hate to admit it, Money and Power do play exceptionally large roles in politics. I think it is an even bigger issue at the federal level. Even though we have an entire chapter on this issue, there will be many references to where these two factors influence legislation, and I rarely see it in a positive way. The "bottle bill" discussed here is a key example of this.

Same-Sex Marriage—

Another issue that came up during the campaign was what my position would be concerning same-sex marriage. Since Iowa had a law forbidding this, I felt an amendment outlawing same-sex marriage was not needed, even though I strongly believe that same-sex marriage conflicts with my Christian convictions. I was wrong about the law being enough.

When an Iowa Judge questioned the constitutionality of this law, that immediately "legalized" same-sex marriage, and within an hour two men were united in "marriage." An injunction stopped further marriages until the Supreme Court made a decision. In the spring of 2009, the Court decided in a unanimous decision that same-sex marriage is permissible. On April 27, the "weddings" began.

Cigarette tax—

One of the most difficult things to know how to legislate is the public's use of tobacco. How many decisions should a government make for the people? This is a Liberal/Conservative issue that we will deal with more extensively, but it plays a major role with the use of tobacco and maybe the other "sin taxes." Tobacco is a legal substance, the farming of which is subsidized by the Federal Government. Is this a good place for us to consider the quote by former President Ronald Reagan? He said, "If you like it, subsidize it, and if you don't like it, tax it."

I feel very strongly about smoking. It killed my Dad, my best friend, and adversely affected the lives of many other people I know and love. I quit when I was 12! I also started that year, but I was a show-off and just did it to get attention. Athletics has always played an important role in all of my decision making. As a youth I dreamt of becoming a professional baseball player. For that reason I chose to never use tobacco or alcohol. Except for two minor youthful lapses, this has remained true for these last fifty-plus years. Also, as a coach and teacher I felt it imperative to not expect kids to exempt themselves from an activity that their coach condoned for himself.

In the political world my original efforts to curb smoking had everything to do with health and kids, and nothing to do with where the additional money would go, or the individual rights infringement. By necessity, this viewpoint changed. It seemed very few, if any, felt or believed the same way. At least the bill went absolutely nowhere in the first year. Some felt all the money should go only for health purposes. The amount of the increase was hotly debated by a variety of groups. Some argued that no tax increase of any kind was acceptable. Others questioned the use of a "sin tax," the timing, and whether the government should be making decisions like this concerning a legal substance. All of these thoughts and arguments had validity. All I cared about was that the product became more expensive so kids wouldn't start and a few others would quit. All that happened was lots of backroom and caucus talk, but no bill was discussed in a committee and brought out for a vote.

So the second year I tried something else. The financial estimating service calculated that a $1 per pack increase would produce $152

M. in additional revenue for the state (they were high, but that isn't the point). They also indicated that a concurrent cut in Commercial Property Tax from 100% of valuation to 85% would cost $146M in reduced tax revenue. This would leave $6M. to be used to educate and help people break the habit. Looked good to me. Statistics show that for every 50 cents a pack of cigarettes increases, 22,000 kids don't start smoking. So this bill would keep 44,000 kids from starting the habit, make our state more competitive with our neighboring states with property taxes (South Dakota is at 85%), provide much needed property tax relief, promote better health in the future, and provide a few million to help those already addicted. But a member of my own party, and a leader in the House, who opposed nearly all tax increases, killed the bill because he said, "It's one-time income and can't be depended upon past the first year." I argued that by increasing the tax almost three times and projecting that sales would decrease by about 1/3 (actually it came down 30% that first year), income revenues would likely be higher continually.

There is a strong inelastic demand curve for necessities, especially "necessities" to which one is addicted. It is incredibly hard to quit smoking. Studies showed that the price per pack would have to go up at least $3 to $4 for the majority of smokers to seriously consider quitting. But the bill was dead because of the power of one leader. A year later, when the bill was passed and the majority had switched to the Democrats, the money all went into the General Fund with no property tax relief, and the income was $36M more than was collected the previous year. These revenues have leveled off $20-30M above the levels collected before the tax increase. See Appendix for a description of Elastic and Inelastic Demand. Also for the actual numbers (Iowa Cigarette Tax Receipts, FY 2006-FY 2011).

One other thing came up in the last week of the session of year two. Remember that there was the 25/25 split at that time. A lot of political posturing and maneuvering takes place in the final weeks of each session. The Senate Republican leadership came up with the following idea and presented it in caucus: We would double the Cigarette Tax to 72 cents per pack and designate the additional revenue to assist Community Colleges. We were told that the Ds would oppose this and we could use this against them for opposing Community Colleges and opposing a tax increase that surveys showed Iowans favored by about

70%. We were warned that "we have to vote unanimously, because if any one didn't, the bill would be pulled immediately."

I didn't like it and said so. First of all it wasn't enough, and once we raised the tax, regardless of how much, it would not be revisited for a number of years. I also said I believed the Ds would support it too. They did, but the bill was killed in the House by the same leader spoken of earlier. This all may have been planned beforehand, I don't know. This whole procedure was one of the most galling in the four years I served. Smoking in Iowa would be the subject of another major controversy for me in the final weeks of what was to be my final session. But that is a story for a bit later. You'll read about it in Chapter 11, The Finale.

Gambling—

Gambling is a major factor in Iowa politics. Iowa is a very liberal gambling state with more ways to gamble legally than any other state. Taxes and fees on gambling are primary and consistent producers of revenue for the Iowa budget. Generally, the Iowa Legislature has been lenient in allowing more gambling. Besides the lottery, there are eighteen major casinos and two others owned by Native Americans. At this writing there are at least four more casino applications pending, and that eighteenth casino was recently constructed in Lyon County.

The big issue that caused all the controversy came from "Touch Play" machines that suddenly appeared in many bars, convenience stores, and some gas stations and restaurants. These machines were very similar to regular slot machines ("one-armed bandits") found in the casinos, except they paid out in certificates, not cash, and had to be redeemed at the counter. There were at least two major problems with these machines. The first was how they came into existence in the first place. Second was the easy access of these machines to minors. In Iowa, one must be 21 to drink alcohol or enter gambling casinos. The placement of these "Touch Play" machines made it nearly impossible to control who used them. This definitely was an expansion of gambling, and we legislators were never given the opportunity to vote for or against them.

Years before, Iowa had chosen to establish a separate Commission on Gaming. This Commission would control the number of gaming licenses issued and answered mainly to the Governor. In an effort to enhance revenues, the "Touch Play" machines were purchased for a pilot program in approximately 50 bars throughout the state. They were phenomenally successful in terms of increased revenue for the state as well as the business establishments. Before anyone in the Legislature knew what had happened, 15,000 machines were located throughout the state, and more were on order. Regardless of popularity, legislators don't like things like this to happen without previous approval and oversight.

Investigations began, testimony was given, legalities were questioned, business operators were heard, and finally a vote was scheduled. This would be a very tough vote for nearly everyone, regardless of party. It was even tough for me even though my campaign speech included, "I will not vote to increase gambling!" A lot of pressure was put on every legislator from a variety of camps. Bars, convenience stores, and restaurants were strongly in favor of the machines. The eighteen casinos, religious organizations, and others opposed to gambling in any way, were also very vocal. Of course, their reasons for being opposed differed.

We legislators were told that the agreement with the machine producers was air tight and we would not be liable if we voted out "Touch Play." After many hours of debate, "Touch Play" was voted out because of the way the machines were introduced. I did vote against them even though many constituents wanted to keep them. I honestly believe that there are more legislators in both houses who favor gambling and would have approved these machines had they been placed only in bars. I really didn't expect my vote to be on the side of the casinos, but they didn't appreciate the additional competition for the gambling dollar.

FRANK

I began my political career by running for mayor of Eldridge, Iowa. With no political background or issues to stand on, my platform was simply "I'll work to make things better." The main concerns were the general demeanor of the city council with the mayor and how things were being done. These relationships (or lack thereof) seemed to catch the weekly paper's headline each week. With encouragement from some key locals, I decided to seek the position.

There was only one public forum with the incumbent. This was sponsored by the local Chamber of Commerce, and there were about 60 people attending. My most distinct memory dealt with the question of individual platforms. After listening to the incumbent, I reflected on my real reason for running. My clear and concise response was, "I want to give you citizens a choice. If you are satisfied with the current direction the city is going, vote for the current mayor. If not, I'm giving you a choice." My qualifications developed from being a coach, administrator, teacher, and group leader with a working knowledge of "Robert's Rules," and placed me in a good position for city leadership.

After being elected by a 2 to 1 margin, I had to learn the job on the go. I made Committee assignments, designating each council person as a liaison for each of the city departments. The operation seemed to run smoothly with limited controversy. I learned quickly that each city council must certify its budgets long before the state actually finalizes its budgets. Eldridge found itself losing budgeted money because of state adjustments and there wasn't any recourse in re-certifying or seeking the opportunity to make changes to address the shortfalls. In spite of this, I am proud to say we did not raise taxes during my tenure as Mayor of Eldridge.

Thinking about going to the Iowa Senate was another story. I sat down with a couple of presently serving Democrat senators to find out what was involved before I committed. This meeting was both insightful and encouraging.

Democratic Party meetings and workshops during the campaign helped me to establish the "ol' stump speech" and to learn the do's and don'ts. Our three main planks would be Education, Jobs, and Health Care. Having 33 years experience in the educational field made me a good spokesperson for what was happening in classrooms and school administration throughout the state. My role as mayor gave me first-hand knowledge of what good paying jobs can do for a community. Also knowing how many of our children do not have access to adequate health care coverage gave me the impetus to seek more information and to speak out with fervor and purpose.

I must also say that I was nervous about the potential of being elected and then not having a particular axe to grind, or flaming issue to push. I also didn't have the foggiest about how to write a Bill! I just thought the Senators would sit down together, discuss the issues, and work out a solution for the betterment of the state. Ignorance may be bliss, but that bliss is temporary!

I attended many meetings and listened to the concerns of special interest groups. Going door-to-door in my district let me hear the constituents' wants and wishes. Many phone calls and notes from friends, relatives, acquaintances, and some strangers apprised me about the myriad of laws that needed writing or changing. It was amazing how many issues, problems, and laws people wanted me to address and change when they knew I was going to run for office!

To quote President George H. W. Bush, "Stay the course," and that's what I did. Education was the number one topic; how would we, as a state, keep our high academic standing in the nation. I had seen many initiatives put into place, some good and some not so good. Schools were being asked to do more and more record keeping and testing. Educators were expected to teach kids the twenty-first century skills needed to be productive and successful. So let's fast forward into the politics of the situation.

When I arrived in Des Moines, the Democratic Caucus was more than excited and upbeat. We had just come from a 21-29 minority to a 25-25 split. I had heard many times how mean the Republicans had been when they were in the majority. They would do their own things, and then tell the Democrats what was going to happen. So I actually thought that this even split would be a good thing as it would make both sides sit down to talk with each other and work together for the best results. It would also keep the far left and far right issues off the table as neither party would allow that to happen. My freshman classmates (two Republicans and five Democrats) met a number of times prior to the start of session. Between the seven of us, we had three educators, four mayors, a fire fighter, retired postal worker, small business owner, and an insurance agent. Yes, I know that adds up to more than seven. Many of us fell into a couple of these categories.

I was put on the Education, State Government, Natural Resources, Human Resources, and Education Appropriations committees. As I got to know many of the Republicans, I found that we could work together on many issues. It seemed that each committee's work was productive, except the one I cared about the most—Education. I found myself frustrated with the lack of any positive progress in this committee. Senator Schoenjahn and I assigned a grade to the committee: an F! Yes, we did a political thing by sending out our grade in a letter to the editor of each newspaper in the state. We didn't mention any names or discuss the problems, but we did mention the lack of cooperative leadership from the other party. May I say that the letter did cause a bit of an uproar, particularly with some Republican senators!

"Don't judge another man until you have walked a mile in his moccasins."

Old Indian Proverb

CHAPTER 2
Republicans vs. Democrats vs. Independents
Conservatives vs. Liberals vs. Moderates

DAVE

Are stereotypes always wrong? I don't think so. Just think how they became stereotypes to begin with. Some people observed things, probably a number of times, and made a determination that "that's the way it is." In this chapter we'll take a look at a number of these stereotypes concerning our political parties and check how valid or invalid they may be.

The three branches of government (Executive, Legislative, Judicial) are all put in place to govern at the Federal, State and Local levels. Now consider how the two-party system has kept all this working. It keeps more people unified with a centralization of purpose. It is hard enough to keep two groups of people focused and on task; multiple parties make it even more difficult. This is one reason why I don't like to see the growth of Independents. Besides being a third party, this group really has no official representation. Oh yes, I know that Lieberman (a former Democrat converted to Independent) from Connecticut is officially an Independent in the Senate. But what is their platform or plan for America? The Republicans and Democrats each have extensive organizations platforms, philosophies, and methods to get things done. They also have the means to get the financial backing necessary to carry out their programs.

So let's examine these two parties, some stereotypes, some history, and what makes each of them successful and such an integral part of America.

Republicans Support:

Smaller Government
Balanced Budgets (What's that?)
Pro Business/Management
Less Regulation (or if you prefer-Deregulation)
Lower Taxes/Less Spending
Strong National Defense
Pro-Life
Tougher Immigration Laws (A Border Fence!)

Democrats Support

More Money for Education
Pro-Union Legislation
Increased Support for Social Programs and the Downtrodden
Higher Minimum Wage
More Equal Civil Rights
Pro-Choice
Global Warming Advocacy—"Going Green"

Here's another belief I have. Democrats are more willing to provide funding for various programs than are Republicans. There is some truth to their "tax and spend" reputation. One problem with the funding is that the Ds leave decisions about how the money is allocated up to the bureaucrats. Rs are more budget conscious and "tighter" but they are more succinct in how the money is distributed. So, one might say, "Let the Ds provide the amounts, and the Rs decide the distribution." That will probably never happen because of the "majority rule" situation. Also, why is everything always a million (or billion) here, and a million-and-a-half there? I never saw a Bill that said, "We need $748,362.54 to complete this project." Everything is rounded off (and usually up). This is another reason why governments are not very efficient.

You may classify the above as accurate, hearsay, stereotypical, or off-base. How about the "fact" that Republicans are automatically Conservative and Democrats are Liberals? Here are a few other "facts" to consider and examine. Catholics tend to be Democrats; so do teachers, social workers, and union members. Business Executives, Protestants, and Farmers tend to be Republicans. Blacks and Hispanics tend to be Democrats, and Jews—Republicans. Check it out. Of course you will always find exceptions, but you will find it intriguing research.

Do you know what you are? Do you even care? Can you make yourself one of the others or is it in your genes? Can/Do you change as you age? Are Republicans Conservative and Democrats Liberal? Is it bad to be a Liberal and good to be a Conservative? How about vice versa? Can one be a Conservative on some issues and a Liberal on others? Or is that the definition of a Moderate?

Here are my answers to these questions, and you may certainly agree or disagree. (Of course you'll be wrong if you disagree!) It's neither good nor bad to be Conservative or Liberal. We need both to make good laws. You have the right to believe whatever way you please. That is what is so great about this country. I do think people can change. Ronald Reagan was a union-leading Democrat; he changed to become one of the most conservative Republican presidents in U.S. history. I also believe there are degrees of conservatism and liberalism. I tend to be very conservative on social issues and more moderate on most others.

Former Iowa Governor Tom Vilsack called me in for a meeting shortly after my primary election victory. I understand he did this with all of the newly elected legislators, regardless of party affiliation. In my estimation, this is a very good idea for any governor or political leader. During that meeting he said, "We can discuss issues from the Left (Liberal) and the Right (Conservative), but we have to legislate in the middle."

He was right (no pun intended). People on the extremes (far left or far right) tend to be neither reasonable nor practical. Legislators must seek common ground and be willing to compromise to produce the best laws. Sometimes we have to pass laws that aren't perfect, but are better than those presently on the books.

Here are a few personal experiences that I hope will cast some light on this subject.

A number of years ago, Republican Representative Fred Grandy decided to run for Governor. Fred was known as a Conservative and asked me to be his Sioux County Chairman for the campaign. Because I was publicly supporting him, I received the following phone call from a lady in the district.

"How can you support a man who favors abortion?"

I disputed the claim that Grandy was pro-abortion and tried to explain it with the following analogy: "Since Roe vs. Wade (1973), any kind of abortion is legal in America. Fred voted to permit abortion only in cases of rape, incest, and life endangerment of the mother. This is about 2% of all the legal abortions performed in the U.S. So 98% of all of the present abortions would become illegal. I would vote for that too, because this is far better than what we have now in my opinion. Don't you agree?"

Her answer was a firm "No!"

Is that being too conservative?

The Iowa Smoking Ban brings forth another scenario. Conservatives ask, "How many decisions should the government make for the people?" "Are we becoming a nanny state?" Moderates or Liberals could say, "Only 18 to 20% of the people smoke; it's a health care issue. And look how well the seat-belt law works! Sometimes we have to make decisions for people that they refuse to make for themselves because of health or safety issues."

Who's right? It was the argument over this issue that ultimately motivated me to leave office. It wasn't just this issue, but it was the "straw that broke the camel's back." I'll tell you that whole story in Chapter 11: The Finale.

In pursuit of a graduate degree in 1982-83 I attended the University of Nebraska/Lincoln. One of the required classes was in the Advanced Theory of Macroeconomics. Professor Peterson, the most liberal person I've ever met, talked a lot about liberal and conservative viewpoints. Not knowing exactly where I would fall on the spectrum, I asked him if there was any instrument to measure whether one was liberal or conservative. After he answered in the negative, I asked if I could prepare one to complete a class requirement. He said I could, and you can see this instrument, "Right/Left/Center?" in the Appendix. If you so choose, follow the instructions to fill it out, and you will then know where you "fit in."

I have administered it over 10,000 times and had some well-known political celebrities complete it. Some refused, even though I promised them I would not publish their results. You will have to talk to me if you want to know who they are and how they scored. But those who completed the instrument added a lot to its validity. It has been proven to be a valid instrument although some changes had to be made from the original. (I even earned an "A" on the assignment!)

The original made reference to party affiliation and degree of Liberal/Conservative leanings. It is just not accurate to say all Democrats are Liberal and Republicans are Conservative. It is accurate to say that there are more liberals in the Democratic Party and more conservatives in the Republican Party. You may reproduce this instrument and use it as much as you choose, because I have no copyright on it and don't want one. It was designed as an educational tool, and that's the way it should be used. The scoring key is also included. I have taken it numerous times in my life and have always been moderate. However, I move closer to the conservative side the older I get, for whatever that is worth. When Frank took it, he scored as a liberal.

Basically, Conservatives want smaller government, less regulation, and less change. Liberals lean toward reform of social institutions and more government intervention.

The media can be very influential, and it is important for you to detect bias. The Wall Street Journal, Fox News, and U.S. News and World Report are known to lean to the conservative viewpoint. In contrast, The Washington Post, CBS News, and Newsweek show a more liberal bias. It is important for you to detect bias in reporting so as to make more accurate evaluations. Listen to both sides and make up your own mind.

Just as America needs two strong political parties, she also needs Liberal as well as Conservative perspective on issues. If too many Liberals prevail in legislation, individual freedom, free markets, expanded immigration, and increased government spending will be evident. If too many Conservatives prevail, the government will be more "hands off" except in national defense, welfare funding will be reduced, and legislation protecting the environment will lessen. Of course this is not an exclusive list of what may or may not happen.

I believe we need open-minded people presenting innovative ideas from BOTH sides, willing to compromise, and writing bills that will help the vast majority of people, while providing a safety net for the underprivileged and minorities. That seems to be extremely tough to get done, and I wish I knew how to thwart the things that stop it.

Don't ever be ashamed or proud of being Conservative, Moderate, or Liberal. That's just the way you believe, and it's okay. It doesn't make you better or worse than anyone else. The problems evolve when one refuses to work with others and insists on his/her own way. Everyone has some good ideas, and we really do need each other. Can you think of a good marriage where the viewpoints of just one of the partners are all that's carried out?

I am a studious reader of God's Word. Many years ago I came across a verse in the Old Testament book of Ecclesiastes. For some reason my liberal friends don't care much for it. Just for fun, why don't you look it up? It's the 2nd verse of Chapter 10. The King James and New International versions are the best for this particular verse. (If you don't want to look it up, turn to the Appendix; it is written out for you.)

FRANK

Prior to my run for the State Senate, I was a registered Republican! Yes, that's right. To tell you the truth, I really didn't know that I was a registered Republican as I typically went to the polls and voted for the person who I felt would do the best job. I didn't look at his or her political affiliation. I wasn't a strong political advocate at all. I was pictured with the "Young Republican" group in my high school yearbook, probably because my girlfriend at the time was in that group as well. I feel that I am basically conservative in nature.

I would love to start my own business. My father was a mason contractor, and I labored for him for more than seven years when I was growing up. At one time after my college graduation, I was applying for teaching jobs and there wasn't much open in the Quad City area. I had just gotten married in the summer of '73, and my wife was employed in the Quad Cities; I knew that I could continue to work for my father and some day take over the family business if I desired. My Dad was a union contractor and I enjoyed the benefits of a good hourly wage. I am pro-choice and I support many of the union issues. I have also spent my entire working life, after college, in education in one form or another. So why did I switch parties?

My son Brian is a firefighter for the City of Davenport. He has been very active in his union. That being said, he was heavily involved in the John Kerry campaign in '04. Remember, I was the mayor of Eldridge at this time, too. As in most campaigns, when the Kerry contingent found out that Brian's Dad was a mayor, they came looking for me to talk about Senator Kerry's platform. The campaign people came to my high school and talked with me about my concerns, so I listened carefully to each of their planks. I found that I agreed with most of Kerry's platform. I thought he shared my beliefs concerning education and would do more for education than what had been done under the Republican regime.

Shortly after my meeting, the Kerry campaign asked me to become a precinct captain. That's when I found out I was a registered Republican. That had to be changed! Prior to caucus, I changed my registration and fulfilled my duties as a precinct captain. That was my first caucus. I truly feel that my beliefs are more in line with the Democrats and probably have been for a long time.

One thing that Dave mentioned is that he is very much behind the two-party system. I agree that the Republicans and Democrats have their platforms very much detailed and in place. I also agree that a third party, whoever that may be, is not in any position to make much of a difference in the political scene. Of course, a third party can and will take votes away from one party or the other. Some say Ross Perot's run took votes away from Kerry. In such a close race, maybe he did. Who knows how many elections were altered to some degree by Ralph Nader?

When I initially sat down with Senators Courtney and Stewart while analyzing the possibilities of becoming a candidate, I realized how much in line I was with the Democratic positions on most issues. I knew I could support and run on the majority of them. I also know that when Dave and I began to discuss issues, we found ourselves agreeing with many of the basic principles, but usually followed different approaches. I believe that when people sit down to discuss issues, and really want to reach some goals, they can solve anything.

"Those who don't study history-are destined to repeat it."

Edmund Burke

CHAPTER 3

History Does Repeat Itself

DAVE

First of all, consider the following facts.

1. When the stock market crashed in 1929, Hoover knew revenues would fall and the budget must be balanced, so he raised taxes! Good Grief! That compounded the problem. An economic rule of thumb that has been successful is to lower taxes and increase spending in a recession, and to balance the budget in recovery times.

2. Kennedy and Reagan both gave massive tax cuts to get out of recession to promote recovery. Both succeeded. Reagan also gave us the biggest tax increase once the recovery was well instituted.

3. Sub-prime, low collateral loans preceded the recession of the late 70's and early 80's. These two mistakes preceded the 2008 recession as well.

4. The national debt has risen EVERY year since 1956. (Yes it went up $18 B in Clinton's best year; see www.publicdebt.treas.gov if you don't believe me.) The national debt went from $5.7 T to $8 T from 2001 to 2005, but the amount of interest the government paid went down from $200 B to $177 B! Even though interest rates didn't fall greatly. Why? The answer is that the Government stopped borrowing as much from the public and borrowed more internally (from

Government agencies like the Social Security Trust Fund and others) and then gave IOU's for the interest instead of paying.

The National Debt will NEVER be paid back, and it doesn't have to be. How does that grab you? See the Appendix for the rationale. Always compare the yearly Deficit to the annual Gross Domestic Product (GDP): the dollar value of all Goods and Services produced within a country in one year. To keep things in perspective, also compare the National Debt to the Total Assets of the United States. For those of you who want to study this more extensively, I have included in the Appendix a number of government tables as well as documents I created while teaching economics. (Tables B-81 and B-89 from the Economic Report of the President; Economic Fact Sheet; Schedule 3: Historical Economic Data.). These will be referred to again in future chapters.

What is imperative is that Americans keep working, producing, trading, and controlling our individual indebtedness. This we must do regardless of which party is in power.

Here are a few comments I believe to be true about America's two-party system. This great country has lasted since 1776 (236 years at this writing), and I think the two-party system has played a major role. No other country in history has lasted that long with the same form of government. Just meditate on what this country has survived, but still remains the strongest and best place to live on Earth:

Four Presidential Assassinations (Lincoln, Garfield, McKinley, Kennedy)

Two Near Impeachments (Johnson and Clinton)

A Civil War that killed more Americans (623,026) than WWI, WWII, Korean War, and Viet Nam Wars combined. (Source: World Almanac)

Lost a War (Viet Nam) and participated in 29 other Wars or Conflicts where service men and women were killed.

Nine Major Stock Market Crashes: 3 in 1929 and 6 worse since then (Source: Dow Jones)

One Presidential Resignation (Nixon)

Numerous Questionable Elections, including 4 where the President didn't win the popular vote: (John Quincy Adams, Rutherford B. Hayes, Benjamin Harrison, and George W. Bush)

Five Depressions, including the Great Depression of the 1930's. Plus 12 Recessions since the '30's, Scandals, Near Assassinations, Organized Crime, Gangs, Drugs, Terrorist Attacks, Murders of National Leaders, and Countless Natural Disasters.

In spite of all this (and you can probably think of some other events) this country has thrived and risen to greatness. This great country's founding fathers had amazing insight as they used the Cornerstones of Capitalism (Appendix) to build an economic system second to none year-in and year-out.

What's so great about the two-party system besides its durability and longevity? "Americans vote their pocketbooks." Is this true or just another speculative stereotype? I believe it to be true. With only two parties, when the economic situation sours, it is easier to switch powers to give the other party a chance. The other party knows what did or didn't work and can make adjustments.

Let's go back to the Republican Herbert Hoover and the start of the Great Depression. He was the only President who hailed from Iowa. He was elected in 1928, and ran for re-election in 1932. The economy was frightful and Franklin Delano Roosevelt, a Democrat, was elected. FDR died in office in 1945 and Harry S. Truman took over. In the midst of a War, America has tended to stay with the man in office. Truman was not a popular President while in office. The Korean "Police Action" was equally unpopular.

Because Truman wasn't eligible to run in 1952, General Dwight D. Eisenhower, a Republican, was chosen over Adlai Stevenson. Eisenhower promised to "go to Korea and end the war." He did. For the most part the 50's were pretty good economic times. We experienced two small recessions and were in one in 1960 when Vice President Nixon faced John F. Kennedy. The people chose our first Catholic president, and the election was disputed, very close, and a switch to the Democrats. Pocketbooks did play a role as Kennedy promised a major tax cut in his "New Frontier."

One of the great American tragedies was the assassination of Kennedy, Nov. 22, 1963. Lyndon Johnson succeeded, and in 1964 the economy was progressing nicely even though the conflict in Viet Nam was accelerating. Johnson's promise of a "Great Society" was greeted with a massive vote to move the House and Senate into even greater Democrat control. Economics is not ALWAYS the biggest factor that causes people to vote Democrat or Republican. As a youth I remember the "Solid South" being Democrat. But in 1964 the Johnson Administration passed the "Civil Rights Act." The Solid South remained "Solid," but now they were Republicans. That's far from the best reason to become a Republican in my estimation.

But let's get back to the 60's. This proved to be the best economic decade since the "Roaring 20's." However, at the close of this decade things were starting to slow down. Interest rates were rising, inflation was climbing, the national debt was escalating because none of the budgets were balanced, and the Vietnamese War was more and more unpopular. Johnson shocked the nation by announcing that he would not seek re-election. This opened the doors for Nixon and Hubert Humphrey. Unhappy people narrowly elected Nixon. By 1972, the '69/'70 recession was over. Interest rates were down from 7.9% to 5.2%. Inflation was down from 5.7% to 3.2% and GDP growth was up from 0.2% to a lusty 5.4%. The war didn't look good, but the pocketbooks spoke, and Nixon won a landslide re-election.

Then came the "shocks of the '70's!" OPEC raised oil from $2.50 a barrel to $35. Gas prices quadrupled and supplies dwindled. We lost the war and treated our returning soldiers shamefully. Watergate exploded, and Nixon was forced to resign or be impeached. Stagflation (High inflation (11%) and no Growth (GDP minus 0.67%) developed. Unemployment hit double figures. Gerald Ford had no chance when he faced Governor Jimmy Carter in 1976. Even though the economy got a little better in the late '70's, the numbers were still bad. By 1980 we had slipped into the worst recession since the Great Depression. This, plus the Iranian Hostage situation, doomed Carter. Ronald Reagan won in a landslide anti-Carter, anti-economy vote. The Republicans also took control of the Senate for the first time since 1955. Reagan was a true optimist, and he instituted the largest tax cut in history. Kennedy/Johnson held the previous record.

The actual recovery began in July, 1982 and by 1984 the people were ready to re-elect the "Deregulation President" in another land slide. Since the economy was still flourishing in '88, Reagan's Vice

President, George Herbert Walker Bush was elected. A small 6-month recession (which Bush would not admit) gave the '92 election to Bill Clinton. The people didn't like the "read my lips" statement by Bush concerning a tax increase and the inconclusiveness of the Kuwait Persian Gulf invasion.

Bill Clinton took over the Presidency during an economic downturn and was the beneficiary of the Dot-Com explosion due to the World Wide Web and the tremendous increase of computers and related technology. These investments caused the stock market to rocket to unknown heights. The '90's proved to be the best economic decade in U.S. history and of course Clinton was re-elected as pocketbooks were full. But interest rates (already in the 8% range) started to rise as inflation crept up in 1999-2000. GDP slipped a little and, in one of the most controversial elections in history, George W. Bush was elected by the Electoral College after losing the popular vote by over a half million votes. Former Clinton V.P. Al Gore won the popular vote but lost the election. (At least he "Invented the Internet!")

There was a short light recession in 2001, and then the economy was very healthy until 2008. Bush was re-elected by over 3 million votes in 2004. However, by the end of 2008 the economy was heading for a deep recession. The Democrats took over the Presidency, the House, and the Senate by substantial margins. This once again substantiates the statement that people do indeed vote their pocketbooks.

Some positive facts about the 2008 election are that it was the first time an African-American was elected President. Obama won with over 50% of the vote, and the excitement of youth was very evident. I have never observed such excitement at an inauguration. The resiliency of America is amazing. Obama inherited a miserable situation globally and at home. At this writing no one knows how deep and how long The Recession will be. Actually, technically, it is quite a short recession but one that is exceptionally weak and slow to recover.

The difference between a recession and a depression is two-fold, encompassing the severity of the down turn and the length. Recessions are less than three years and the Leading Economic Indicators (see the Appendix) turn negative. The main items evident in a depression are high unemployment, many business failures, low or no growth in GDP, possible inflation, high interest rates, and very low consumer confidence.

Normal economic goals are inflation under 3%, unemployment under 5%, GDP growth at 3% or higher, and low interest rates under 6%.

Globally, Obama faced ending the war in Iraq and Afghanistan, immigration woes, a weak dollar, financial markets in a tailspin, and many other countries in recession. His task was/is most difficult. Now here is what I mean about why the two-party system is great. The Democrats controlled the Presidency, House, and Senate with substantial majorities. They had the power and the necessity to produce. Since the war wasn't over in less than two years, it was no longer "Bush's war," it became "Obama's war."

Since the economy wasn't well into recovery, the 33 Senators (and most of them Democrats) up for election in 2010 were in jeopardy. The 233-202 advantage held by the Democrats in the House became a Republican majority as at least 60 seats were gained. The Ds maintained a narrow margin in the Senate though they lost 6 seats. The minority party (Rs) had the opportunity to observe what didn't seem to work in those first two years and now have had two more, with the opportunity to watch the Ds try something else. If what they try doesn't satisfy the people, and the economy doesn't rebound, look for another switch in power in the 2012 election back to the Rs. You can also bank on the reality of a new Republican President if the pocketbooks don't fill up.

Iowa Caucus System

Maybe this is a good time to apprise you of how the Iowa two-party system works. In lieu of a Primary Election where a popular vote determines the winner, Iowa uses a system of 1774 precincts that meet in party caucus to decide which Presidential candidate will win Iowa. Since January, 1972 Iowa has been the first state to start the Presidential selection process. New Hampshire is always the first to conduct a Primary.

FRANK

The Democratic Caucuses:

My first caucus process was in 2004 when I got involved discussing the upcoming election with my son, Brian. Remember, Brian is a firefighter and a strong union proponent. Both Brian and I became strong supporters of Senator John Kerry in his Presidential bid. As the Mayor of Eldridge, I was called by the Kerry campaign to see if I would be a precinct captain. I wasn't aware of what my role might be, but I decided to take on the role. In the city of Eldridge, we have two voting precincts, and I represented Precinct 1. Kerry was running against Dick Gephardt, Howard Dean, and John Edwards for the '04 Presidential nomination. Negative campaign ads attacking each of the top two front runners (Gephardt and Dean) soured the voters on them, and a last minute decision by Kerry to put all of his remaining money in Iowa proved to be wise as Senator Kerry went on to win Iowa and then New Hampshire.

The Process:

The process used by the Democrats is more complex than the Republican Party caucus process. Each precinct divides its delegate seats among the candidates in proportion to caucus goers' votes. Participants indicate their support for a particular candidate by standing in a designated area of the caucus site, forming a preference group. An area may also be designated for undecided participants. Then, for roughly 30 minutes or more, participants try to convince their neighbors to support their candidates. Each preference group might informally deputize a few members to recruit supporters from other groups and, in particular, from among the undecided. Undecided participants might visit each preference group to ask its members about their candidate.

After the 30 minutes has passed, the electioneering is temporarily halted and the supporters for each candidate are counted. At this point, the caucus officials determine which candidates are viable. Depending on the number of county delegates to be elected, the viability threshold is 15% of the attendees. For a candidate to receive any delegates from a particular precinct, he or she must have the support of at least the percentage of participants required by the viability threshold. Once viability is determined, participants have roughly another 30 minutes to realign: the supporters of unviable candidates may find a viable candidate to support, join together with supporters of another unviable candidate to secure a delegate for one of the two, or choose to abstain. This realignment is a crucial distinction of caucuses in that (unlike a primary) being a voter's second candidate of choice can help that candidate.

When the voting is closed, a final head count is conducted, and each precinct apportions delegates to the county convention. These numbers are reported to the state party, which counts the total number of delegates for each candidate and reports the results to the media. Most of the participants go home, leaving a few to finish the business of the caucus; each preference group elects its delegates, and then the groups reconvene to elect local party officers and discuss planks for the platform.

The delegates chosen by the precinct then go to a later caucus, the county convention, to choose delegates to the district convention and the state convention. Most of the delegates to the Democratic National Convention are selected at the district convention, with the remaining ones selected at the state convention. Delegates to each level of convention are initially bound to support their chosen candidate, but can later switch in a process very similar to what goes on at the precinct level; however, as major shifts in delegate support are rare, the media declares the candidate with the most delegates on the precinct caucus night the winner, and relatively little attention is paid to the later caucuses.

2004 Democratic Process:

In January, '04 the meetings ran from 6:30 p.m. until approximately 8:00 p.m. There was a turnout of about 124,000 caucus-goers. The county convention occurred on March 13, the district convention on April 24, and the state convention on June 26. Delegates could and did change their votes based on further developments in the race; for instance, in '04 the delegates pledged to Dick Gephardt, who left the race after the precinct caucuses, chose a different candidate to support at the county, district, and state level.

The number of delegates each candidate receives eventually determines how many state delegates from Iowa that candidate will have at the Democratic National Convention. Iowa sends 56 delegates to the DNC out of a total of 4,366.

Of the 45 delegates who were chosen through the caucus system, 29 were chosen at the district level. Ten delegates were at-large delegates, and six were 'party leader and elected official' (PLEO) delegates; these were assigned at the state convention. There were also 11 other delegates, eight of whom were appointed from local Democratic National Committee members; two were PLEO delegates and one was elected at the state convention.

2008 Process:

The January '08 precinct caucus was much the same as in '04. I supported Gov. Tom Vilsack in the beginning of the campaign after working with him for two years as a State Senator. After he dropped out, I began to be courted by Senators Joe Biden and Barack Obama. I was fortunate enough to have personal visits with Sen. Biden's son and his sister right in Eldridge. Gov. Bill Richardson visited Eldridge as did Sen. Obama. I remember attending a state conference in South Carolina and being called by Sen. Obama requesting a meeting to discuss his platform. Since I worked in the public education sector, I told him that I needed to hear his platform planks regarding education, and just what he stood for in this area. He told me that when I got back home he would have a staffer call on me and discuss his platform. I don't really remember hearing much from his staffer; I felt that I did all the talking and I told the staffer my platform. I do remember the staffer telling me that Sen. Obama was on the same page as I and that he would certainly appreciate my support.

That same week, Sen. Obama held a press conference and discussed his platform on public education. Much to my surprise, it was almost word for word to that of what I had said to the staffer one week earlier. Are you surprised to hear that the next day I called the Obama campaign headquarters and told them I would endorse the Senator, but I needed him to stop in Eldridge and do a fund raiser for me. A couple of weeks went by and I was called by the Obama campaign. They told me that the Senator was going to be driving through the area, and if I could get a place for a fund raiser, he would stop by for an hour and help me out. Senator Obama ended up winning Iowa with 38% of the delegates. John Edwards was second with 30%, and Hillary Clinton took third with 29%.

This past caucus in 2012 was less eventful due to President Obama running for his second term. Scott county Democrats held one large convention in Bettendorf; each precinct was able to break out into their own smaller group to discuss the platform and go through the administrative tasks of selecting district and county delegates. President Obama appeared via the web and gave an uplifting speech to his constituents.

DAVE

To be expected, the Republicans and the Democrats conduct their Caucuses differently. Frank discussed how the Ds do it, and I'll apprise you of the Rs' way. But first it's important to say why Iowa enjoys being first. With only 3 million people and 99 counties, the population is spread out and the rural areas are important. So the Presidential candidates, all of whom think it imperative to get off to a good start, spend copious amounts of time and money in Iowa. Because of the unique small group personal contact motif, many small state Governors (Jimmy Carter in '76, Bill Clinton in '92, Mike Huckabee '08) get great media coverage, name recognition, and an opportunity to present and practice their messages and ideas. It's been a launching pad for many. Had you heard a lot about Barack Obama before he won in Iowa?

The Republican Process:

In Iowa, one must choose which party caucus one wants to attend. You must register as an R or a D to take an active part, and you can't participate in both. Youth, the press, and other visitors are welcomed. Both parties start the platform writing process in the caucuses, but the voting and delegate selection is different. Even though the caucuses are held every two years, it's the ones during the "Presidential years" that get the attention.

In 1980 the Rs decided to use a "straw vote" of those in attendance to decide the winner. Each candidate has a designated representative that gives a short (5 minutes or so) speech in support of him or her. I was that speaker for Mitt Romney in both '08 and again in '12. Each person is given a paper ballot and the vote is taken. The vote is not binding because the county delegates are chosen and they are not bound to vote for the straw vote winner. I don't like that aspect but it's amazing what an effect that vote has on the candidates. It really "gives them a boost" or "deflates their balloon" as they move on to the primary in New Hampshire. Over the years, many candidates who have done poorly in the Iowa Caucus immediately drop out of the race.

Following are the Iowa Caucus results since 1972:

Democrats

1972   Ultimate winner George McGovern finished 3rd (23%) to Edmund Muskie and "Uncommitted (both at 36%)

1976   Jimmy Carter finished 2nd (28%) to "Uncommitted" (very popular with D's at 37%) This proved to be a very significant "win" for Carter.

1980   Jimmy Carter (59%) Ted Kennedy (31%)

1984   Winner Walter Mondale (49%)

1988   Michael Dukakis finished 3rd (22%) to Dick Gephardt (31%) and Paul Simon (27%)

1992   Bill Clinton finished 4th (3%) behind Tom Harkin (76%), "Uncommitted" (12%), and Paul Tsongas (4%)

1996   Bill Clinton (96%)

2000 Al Gore (63%) wins over Bill Bradley (37%). (I was a D that night because I thought George W. would win handily and I wanted Bill Bradley to win. I re-registered as an R the next morning for fear of dying as a Democrat! Sorry about that Frank.)

2004 John Kerry (38%) wins over John Edwards (32), Howard Dean (18%), Dick Gephardt (11%), and Dennis Kucinich (1%)

2008 Barack Obama (38%) wins over John Edwards (30%), and Hillary Clinton (29%)

2012 Barack Obama (98%) wins over that old nemesis "Uncommitted" (2%)

Republicans

1972 Richard Nixon in a landslide

1976 Winner Gerald Ford (45%) over Ronald Reagan (43%)

1980 Ronald Reagan finishes 2nd (30%) to George H.W. Bush (32%) and 5 others

1984 Ronald Reagan unopposed

1988 George H. W. Bush is 3rd (19%) to Bob Dole (37%), and Pat Robertson (25%)

1992 George H. W. Bush unopposed

1996 Bob Dole (26%) wins over Pat Buchanan (23%) and 6 others

2000 George W. Bush (41%) wins over Steve Forbes (31%) and 3 others

2004 George W. Bush unopposed

2008   John McCain finishes 4th (13%) to Mike Huckabee (34%), Mitt Romney (25%), Fred Thompson (13%) and 3 others

2012   Mitt Romney finishes 2nd to Rick Santorum (both at 25%) and 5 others. The night of the Caucus it was announced that Romney won by 11 votes. A recount revealed a 38-vote loss. This, plus other controversies and results will make some major changes in the Iowa system for 2016.

"Because that's where the power is."

John F. Kennedy
(when asked why he wanted to be president)

CHAPTER 4

Money—Power—Corruption

DAVE

Unfortunately, these three terms seem to be playing an increasingly big role in the political arena, as well as other aspects of our life.

What makes a politician powerful? There may be a number of things, but tenure and access to money are two of the biggest. Very few, if any, first term legislators are voted into the power positions. The two most powerful slots are Speaker of the House, and Senate Majority Leader. Close behind are the Majority Leader of the House and the President of the Senate. Next come the Minority Leaders in both the House and the Senate. All of these positions are won in each individual party caucus by a majority vote.

The potential leaders usually make a few phone calls, speak individually with caucus members, and let a few influential people know of their interest in leadership. (It reminded me a little of when we were teenagers and wanted that certain girl to know we were interested, but didn't want to appear too anxious or obvious.) Each party also has about five or six Assistant Leadership positions, including the "party whip." He or she is the person who finds out which way each member is leaning on individual bills, and may even apply a little pressure to vote one way or the other. The other Assistant Leaders help mentor rookies and make contributions to the legislative agenda and do planning for the party.

So you can see it stands to reason that some tenure and experience are prerequisites for leadership positions. The other normal leadership qualities of communication skills, intelligence, and drive complete the picture. To get and hold a power position, the leader must be capable of raising huge sums of money. Money is a necessity today to win elections. During a leader's term, the number of seats gained or lost in elections is more important than the quality of legislation passed or not passed. Remember, power comes from being in the majority. So party leaders must fill the coffers or risk defeat in more ways than one. One can continually notice the importance of money in political campaigns, because the press will always compare how much the candidates have in the bank.

FRANK

Money is a huge issue when running for office. I mentioned earlier just how much money was spent on my first race for the Senate. My re-election bid wasn't any different. There was no primary, but the general election was highly contested. I actually thought reelection would be a little easier. It was in a few cases across the state, but not in mine. In reality, I needed even more money and I needed a larger investment of time. Media ads are incredibly expensive. I actually spent $250,000 on my re-election bid. (Isn't that ridiculous for a $25,000 a year job?!)

Besides the leadership positions, the Committee Chairs also carry some weight. They can pretty well allow or stop any bill they choose. However, if it "comes down from the top," the Governor and Majority Leaders usually prevail. I found out much more about this when the Ds took over the majority in my last two years. I was selected as Chair for the important Education Appropriations Committee. The attention given this position was overwhelming. Of course, Education commands close to 60% of the budget, and that's a big slice of the pie. I became familiar with all three Regent Presidents and enjoyed discussing education issues with them.

I was invited to attend football games at both Iowa State and the University of Iowa and sit in the President's suite. Mind you, I did purchase my own tickets to all the games, and I was able to purchase one more ticket for a friend. It was exciting to watch the games from a terrific position, but even more important was the friendship and collaboration with each educational leader. I felt honored to talk with them and let them know that I was extremely interested in making our Regents the best they could be without pitting one against the other. I had my own impression of each of our Universities and thought that each one had its own identity. I found myself getting more and more information from the Presidents, and I believed that they were working hard to make their institution the best it could be.

As Chairman of Ed. Approps. I felt it necessary to make sure that my counterpart (Republican Ranking Member Senator Nancy Boettger) was made aware of what was going on with regard to who was going to get money and why. I also wanted to make sure I knew what her priorities were, and I wanted to see if I would be able to get some of those accomplished. That is how I worked, and I would continue to do so. Dave, as Ranking Member on the Education Committee, also made it easier for me to get support as we discussed everything openly. We agreed on most things and even when we disagreed we supported and respected each other's views. I had the power as chairman to take any suggestion or leave it. I had the votes and the power to pass any bill, but I wanted to be fair and work across the aisle to get the best things done. I feel that the majority of issues worked that way, but the final vote on the Appropriations Bill always got political, meaning that it would be along party lines. I enjoyed the power and prestige that being chairman brought, but I also wanted to be respected for my work ethic, fairness, and the ability to work across the aisle to get what was best for Iowa's variety of schools and colleges. I think that the experiences I encountered in the first two years enabled me to work the way I did when we won the majority.

DAVE

Some people really seem to enjoy the feeling of Power. I must admit, sometimes it is advantageous to either have it or at least have access to it. Think of the statement, "It's not what you know, but who you know." Unfortunately, I'm finding this to be more valid the older I get. I don't particularly like it, but it's true. Here are a few personal examples.

As a State Senator, I had ready access to the Governor, Senators Grassley and Harkin, and our five Federal Representatives. If I emailed, wrote, or called them, I could expect a response the same day. So remember, if you have an immediate problem, (such as passports, visas, immigration issues, licenses, etc.), get in touch with your State Senator and/or Representative. They can and will help in most all cases.

I'm a St. Louis Cardinal fan. Both Dot and I love to watch baseball and visit St. Louis for some games. Good tickets can be hard to come by because the Cards are always a fun team to watch and are usually in contention. (Cubs fans, stop drooling!) I have a friend with access to great lower level box seats close to first base. I have to pay over $50 apiece for them, but I can get four of them for whatever series I want to see. I can't tell you how many free tickets I've received over the years because of knowing some major league players. Unfortunately, all of them have retired, and we're getting nosebleeds at most of the games we attend now!

Just because I served in the Senate, there are a number of people who want me to "lobby" for their special interest. I have never been turned down by a sitting Senator when requesting some time to discuss an issue. This is true with Senators on both sides of the aisle. Is ready access a form of Power? I think so. The same holds true for getting information in the media. It seems that newspapers, radio, and television all have space for those with a title before their names.

Politicians, in order to achieve positions of authority or power, must listen and cater to their constituents. Never forget to contact them when you have a need. "Constituent Care"– two words that motivate each office holder. If you are traveling to the Capitol or to Washington, D.C., be sure to contact your Senator. There are souvenirs, tours, tickets, pictures, and a variety of things that will be made available to you. Many times you can visit your Senator in his/her office and get an autographed picture on the Capitol steps. Let them use their "Power" to assist you. As was stated before, one of the best things about holding office was meeting and greeting constituents when they came to the Capitol. Never forget that we were elected as servants of the people. It was/is an honor and a privilege to serve.

As this narrative is being written in 2008, there is an extreme example of Power being used in the Iowa Senate. A huge issue in Iowa, as is mentioned at other times in this book, is the "Gay Marriage" situation.

The Iowa Legislature had passed a "Defense of Marriage" Law in 1998. Some felt this law wasn't strong enough so an effort was made to make Gay Marriages unconstitutional. It takes two successive Legislative Sessions, with both Houses passing and the Governor signing, to bring any Constitutional amendment to a vote of the people. This almost came to pass in the spring of 2004. The Rs controlled both the House and the Senate in those years. The call for the Referendum passed both houses in 2003 but failed in the Senate in 2004. So it was a subject of proposed legislation and discussion for all of the four years I served. But since the Ds were in the majority we could never get it debated, or even brought up on the floor. In a unanimous 2009 decision, the Iowa Supreme Court ruled that the Iowa law was unconstitutional, and gay marriages became legal. Iowa is one of 5 states allowing gay marriage. The other 4 are Connecticut, Massachusetts, New Hampshire, and Vermont. Mainly because of this decision, 3 of the 9 Supreme Court Justices were voted out of office in the November, 2010 election. The Rs regained the majority in the House and narrowed the Senate margin to 24-26. Some of this gain by the Rs may be attributed to the people's unrest over the issue.

In spite of the fact that every state that has held a referendum on this issue has refused to permit same-sex marriages, and 41 states now prohibit it (4 other states do permit civil unions), one man in Iowa has the power to keep the issue from moving forward. As the majority leader in the Senate, he, and he alone, decides what bills will reach the floor of the Senate for debate. In his defense, he believes that it is a civil rights issue and this significant portion of the population should not be denied the right to marry. Whether you agree or disagree with the principles of the issue, this is an example of real POWER. (If this issue is resolved before this book goes to the publisher, I'll inform you as to what happened.)

FRANK

One of the first experiences I found disturbing occurred during my first year in the Senate. The seven of us in the freshman class (we called ourselves the "Super Seven") wanted to write a special bill that all of us could support. We really wanted it to pass in a bi-partisan way. Well, we got the bill written but it never got brought up in committee. We couldn't get the two Co-Chairs to reach any agreement. I remember sitting in Room 42 with the Education Co-Chairs and three of my freshmen brothers. I remember talking to these leaders and asking them if we were going to move any bills at all this year. One of the leaders answered, "I'll bring up one of your bills if you'll bring up one of ours." I asked which bills he wanted. Unfortunately, I couldn't support what he wanted.

I asked him if we could bring up the freshman bill and his comment was, "No, the Democrats will get the credit." All seven of us had signed on as authors of the bill; I told him that it was written in a bi-partisan manner, and he could have one of his Republican freshmen floor manage it. His response was, "The Democrats will still get the credit." I then asked "What is wrong with the bill?" He said, "Nothing, it's a good bill, but the Democrats will get the credit." I was flabbergasted and totally upset (as were the other freshmen), that this GOOD bill was being held up because the Democrats were supposedly going to get the credit.

Power is also evident at the end of each session. Leaders from both chambers discuss with the Governor just what needs to get completed before the end of the session. Once the details begin to filter back, each caucus is given the information for discussion, arguments, and debate. The first two years it was amazing how things went down with the Senate in a tie and with the House being lead by the Rs, and the Governor being a D. The last couple of weeks we saw the leaders from both sides get together to discuss options, work out compromises, and reach final agreement. The last two years were the same, except there were fewer leaders making the decisions because one party had control. One would think that it would be easier to come up with the final decisions, but I felt that this time was as tough or tougher than the time before. With power comes the responsibility to stand up for the decisions and take on all the nay-sayers. Are we addressing all of our constituents and party affiliates? Maybe even more important, how will the campaign donors react? And one more thing, I found much more infighting within our own caucus.

DAVE

I alluded to the fact that more bad things (excessive gifts, corruption) happen at the Federal level. I think this is due to the sheer volume of money and people who are involved. (100 Senators, 435 Representatives, and countless Lobbyists.)

The only corruption I was aware of in my four years in Des Moines involved the Central Iowa Employment and Training Consortium (CIETC) Scandal. It had all of the ingredients: money, sexual allegations, crooked politicians, conspiracy, power, fraud, intrigue, secrecy, and payoffs. CIETC was a job training company in central Iowa. Below is a brief recap of what happened and who was involved. (To read more extensively, Google 'CIETC Scandal' and/or call up news articles.)

The scandal involved some members from the Des Moines City Council, plus board members and executives of CIETC. A state audit first detected exorbitant salaries and bonuses being paid to executives at CIETC. These salaries and bonuses approached $400,000 annually. Some questioning and research revealed illegal use of Federal and State funds. Numerous indictments produced evidence that sent a half dozen to serve prison terms. Many received major fines, lost their jobs, and were forced to resign from various Boards and Councils. Eventually, CIETC went through a name change and was subsequently closed down. This caused many hardships for those needing job training and for other Job Service Agencies across the state.

Once again, I think Power played the major role in this scandal. People did illegal things because they had been in a "Power Position" for some length of time and found a way to circumvent rules and the law. Bigger isn't always better.

So must we say that Money, Power, and Corruption are all bad? We would probably agree that Corruption is always bad, but the other two have many positives. When you think about it, both are necessities. My Mom always told me, "Don't make major decisions based solely on money. It's a necessity, but if money determines your ultimate decision, you are in for major disappointments. You can't buy happiness." Remember what the Bible says, "The LOVE of money is the root of all kinds of evil." (1 Tim. 6:10). It doesn't say money is the root, it says the 'love' of money.

It's not how much you have, it's how you got it and what you do with it. Some of the richest people in the world are actors, actresses, and professional athletes. Eighty percent of their marriages wind up in divorce. Is there a lesson in that statistic?

Is a certain amount of Power necessary to get things done? I think so. In politics, power comes from numbers, the ability to raise money, and the earned reputation of getting positive things done. Certain offices have more power than others. Governor, Majority Leader, Speaker of the House, President, and Committee Chair are the Power positions at the state level. It's the use or abuse of Power that creates or averts problems.

"Better the devil you know than the devil you don't."

Author unknown

CHAPTER 5

Candidate Selection

DAVE

What are the personal qualities you want in a politician? When considering who to vote for, how do you rank the following?

Gender	Voice	Race
Nationality	Honesty	Money
Integrity	Physique	Age
Education	Health	Clothes
Religion	Energy	Family
Communication skills	Work experience	Common sense
Personal friendship	Name recognition	Party
TV appearance	Leadership ability	Marital record
Recommendations	Reputation	Tainted past

Previous elections

Did I miss some? Which of these never enter your mind, and which of these strongly influence your vote? Which of these were the key factors in getting President Obama elected? Do party leaders select potential candidates to run for office the same way you select the person for whom you vote? I hope so, but I don't think so.

Party leaders want someone who will win. What is required to produce that winner? Name recognition, money, willingness to work, a good reputation or untainted past, and balancing the ticket.

Here are some names from past elections for your reflection and analysis. George W. Bush, John F. Kennedy, Thomas Eagleton, Bill Clinton, Ronald Reagan, Dan Quayle, Sarah Palin, Barack Obama, and Edmund Muskie. Some of these overcame "adversity" and were elected, while others either lost or suffered continual ridicule whether it was deserved or undeserved. Why? What's important in an elected official?

It may sound strange for a lifelong Republican to say this, but I was proud of our country when we elected Barack Obama. Did I vote for him? Nope. But this great country elected a black man about 150 years after we had fought our bloodiest war over what basically was a race issue. The other leading candidate was a woman, Hillary Clinton. I believe that says a great deal about progress, change, and equality.

Two interesting quotes come to mind. One produced fear in my heart and the other is fraught with irony. Here are the stories behind these quotes.

A number of years ago I taught a required course for prospective teachers. It was Human Relations and involved cultural study. Rev. Floyd Brown, a black man originally from Missouri, always spoke to the classes representing the black perspective. We became good friends over the years and shared many personal feelings. Both of us were young adults in the 1960's and were very aware of civil rights issues. Floyd had been a "black power activist." Talking about the possibility of a black or a woman being elected President, the good pastor said, "We will elect a woman before we elect a black."

I asked him, "Why?"

"Because a black man will be assassinated!" was his reply. That's a frightening thought that I've never forgotten. Thank the Lord it didn't come true. I talked to candidate Obama about it when he visited Iowa while campaigning. He said every precaution was being taken. To my knowledge there have been no attempts on his life.

The other quote I heard from a black man during a television interview. I'm sorry, but I didn't know him, and I may not quote him exactly. In talking about Obama and the possibility of his election, the man said, "This election is not and should not be about race, but it is time for us to have a black President." So, should race, gender, or whatever other characteristic you choose, be what determines your vote?

As I stated before, voting, whether it is for a candidate, or as a legislator, can be difficult. Have you been thinking about why you voted the way you did in the last election?

When I was asked to consider running in the Iowa District 2 Primary for the Senate position, the three Sioux County Republican Party leaders told me, "We want someone to be a strong voice for NW Iowa, someone who will work to get things done. Don't be afraid to work with the other side to accomplish goals. We need someone who will listen."

I had to run against a man with ten years experience who also held a leadership position in the majority party caucus. He was about the same age as I and was a long time businessman in Orange City, the third largest community in District 2. I was chosen to challenge him because I had good name recognition in Orange City, due to 25 years of teaching and coaching at Northwestern College. My home in Sioux Center, the second largest community in the district, was another plus. I had lived my entire life in the district. He hadn't.

My opponent was not particularly popular in Lyon County, and it was felt Plymouth County would be a tossup. My being a former high school teacher was also considered a plus. That did prove to be beneficial as I received many educators' votes.

Suffice it to say that the plan worked. I carried Orange City, Sioux Center, and my home town of Alton in winning Sioux County by a narrow margin. I lost Plymouth County by 11 votes and carried Lyon County by a big margin.

Party leaders always have a pretty good idea of who in their own party, and in the opponent's party, are vulnerable at election time. This is important because many dollars are directed, or not directed, to campaigns where a victory can be accomplished, or a loss averted.

Remember, leaders are mostly concerned about numbers that produce a majority. Leaders are also knowledgeable about which candidates are involved in a primary. The quote at the beginning of this chapter has great significance to leaders.

As my primary race was progressing, the majority leader at that time placed a call to a Sioux County party leader. In essence, it went like this. "Who is this Mulder? Has he got a chance?"

When told it was a possibility, he said, "Well, just make sure you send me a Republican!" Leaders want numbers, and they want followers. They are not particularly enamored with rebels. In fact, the threat of creating a primary can and may be used to keep a rebel member in line. When leaders lose numbers they are soon replaced.

If you want to know how a particular race is viewed from within the party, watch the money trail. If lots of "party money" is funneled into a race, especially late in the campaign, one can tell how important and how close the race is becoming. Of course, you can check finance funding for any candidate on the State Legislative Website—www.legis.state.ia.us. You'll be surprised at how much information can be obtained at that website during the Sessions and in the interim.

During the campaign a number of debates were conducted throughout the district. The basic differences between us were on Education, Term Limits, and how the district was represented. I can't say definitively why I won, but I did. Neither of us ran a negative campaign, for which I'm thankful. I hate negative and nasty campaigns. Unfortunately, many times negativity seems to be successful.

FRANK

You saw the list of characteristics at the beginning of this chapter that may come to mind when considering a candidate. The biggest one that brought my name to the top of the list was name recognition. I, too, am in public education and have served as a coach and teacher. I had also been elected mayor of the small town of Eldridge and was in the third year of my term when approached to run for the senate.

Anyone interested in running for public office must take a hard look at all of the ramifications of serving at the state level. I remember the initial contact as if it were yesterday. A retired elementary principal I knew well came into my office at school and closed the door behind him. He said, "Hear me out before you say anything!" I really didn't know what was coming, but I had great respect for him after working with him for a number of years. He said, "A number of us have been discussing the Iowa Senate, and you and another principal are at the top of our list. We want you to consider running."

I knew the other fella was a recently retired principal and that he had already gone to Des Moines to "test the waters." When he returned he was no longer interested in the position. My friend strongly encouraged me to give it a battle. I didn't know much about my potential Republican opponent, other than that he was a farmer from the western portion of the district. He had been previously elected to the House of Representatives and then moved on to the vacant Senate seat. Unfortunately for him, District 42 was redistricted, as is done every 10 years to assure equal representation for the districts, so he only served a two-year term in the Senate and then had to run again.

But before facing him I had a Democratic Primary to prepare for. The Democratic candidate who had run two years previously was again in the race. He had lost by just over 1000 votes after entering the campaign at a very late date, and he felt he hadn't had sufficient time to get his message out.

Now it was my turn to make the trip to Des Moines to gain some knowledge and expertise. I visited with some sitting Senators and came back to Eldridge excited about filing my papers and starting the campaign. I immediately called my primary opponent to let him know it would be "a clean fight." I told him that, if he won, I would give him my full cooperation to help him win the seat in November. I also told him that I expected the same from him.

I was told that $150,000 would be needed to win the race. I had won the mayoral position by an overwhelming margin and had spent a mere $500! I surely didn't think I'd need so much money to run for the senate. I would find out much later just how much it took to win the primary and then general elections. That was a real eye opener!

In planning the campaign, I felt confident about the local school district but knew hard work would be needed in Clinton county and a small portion of rural Scott county.

DAVE

Would you vote for a person who made the following statement? "The streets of our country are in turmoil. The universities are filled with students rebelling and rioting. Communists are seeking to destroy our country. Russia is threatening us with her might, and the Republic is in danger. Yes, danger from within and without. We need law and order. Yes, without law and order, our nation cannot survive. Elect us and we shall restore law and order."

Who do you think said that and when? Take a guess and then look in the Appendix.

It can be very difficult to evaluate a person on what he or she says. Campaign periods are getting longer and longer. Good Grief! Representatives never stop campaigning for the next election. Gubernatorial candidates start with "exploratory committees" at least two years in advance, and Presidential "wannabees" begin even sooner. Name Recognition is the magic phrase. How do you get it? Movie stars used to exclaim that any publicity is good publicity. Is that true for politicians as well? I don't think so. Gary Hart comes to mind and, more recently, John Edwards. You can probably think of others. Hard work, media exposure, travel, meetings, interviews, mailings, press releases, pictures, billboards, party support, and of course, the money to do it all, is what everyone tries. Some are "lucky" because of fame garnered from previous private jobs, the military, or well-known families. The Bush's, Kennedy's, Ronald Reagan, and Dwight Eisenhower are all examples of this.

Candidate selection comes down to many things doesn't it? When I analyzed the fifteen senators elected in my four years, here's the breakdown. Two moved up from the House. I was definitely the oldest at 66, and no other had reached 60. Several were in their 30's and at least three were former mayors. Volunteerism was a characteristic of nearly all of the candidates, and four of us were former teachers. Thirteen men and two women won. All of us were married, but one was divorced and another experienced the tragic separation through death. The divorcee was a single dad with custody of three kids, and he did marry a wonderful lady at the close of our first term. All were effective communicators, successful in private life, unafraid of tackling tough issues, and competitive. Each had at least one particular area of expertise, and all cared deeply for our State. I think the vast majority of us wanted to work together, but that is much more difficult than any of us realized. Re-election, caucus pressure, constituent concerns, and some basic party differences cause the difficulties.

I hope this chapter helps you the next time you select a candidate to vote for. I hope, too, that you will become more involved in encouraging and selecting candidates to run for public office, and also consider serving yourself.

Dave Mulder Gallery

Here I am with Presidential candidate Barak Obama when he visited the Capitol. He's signing a picture for me.

Dot and I met with Presidential candidate John McCain when he visited Sioux Center on the campaign trail.

*One real highlight was sharing the banquet table with former
Secretary of State Madeline Albright. We exchanged a few letters discussing
the Iraq war. A great lady!*

*I was Mitt Romney's Sioux County leader in 2008. I got to spend considerable
time with him and continue to support him for President.
Chose a great verse, didn't he?*

Senate President Jack Kibbe let me 'take the chair' in the Senate one day. It made me nervous, but it sure was fun. Secretary of the Senate, Mike Marshall is giving me some guidance.

Governor Chet Culver did become a friend.

Former Presidential Candidate (1972) George McGovern visited Northwestern College. It was my good fortune to travel to Sioux Falls to pick him up. What a gentleman and humanitarian!

This little rascal is Shawn Johnson, the gold medalist and Olympic star. It was a privilege to meet her when she visited the Capitol.

"A true friend is one soul in two bodies."

Aristotle

"The only way to have a friend is to be one."

Emerson

CHAPTER 6

The Freshman Class

FRANK

The November 2004 election was history, and the Iowa State Senate was into a historic even split at 25. This had happened before but not for a long time. All of us were excited to start the new job and represent our districts. The Democrats had a tremendous election, picking up 4 seats and replacing the 21-29 Republican advantage of the previous two years.

The class of '05 brought in seven new legislators. Five were Ds and two were Rs. The Ds all came from the eastern side of the state. Jeff Danielson was a Cedar Falls firefighter. Tom Hancock was a retired postal worker and volunteer fire fighter from Dubuque County. Brian Schoenjahn was a soon-to-be-retired social studies teacher from Strawberry Point. Tom Rielly was an insurance businessman from Oskaloosa. I was the other Democrat, and of course Dave was one of the Republicans. The other one was Brad Zaun. He owned a small hardware store and was the mayor of Urbandale. Brad's was the most expensive senate race in the state as he spent over $400,000 and his opponent over $500,000. (Remember, that was for a job that had a salary of $22,700 at the time.)

I didn't know any of these fine men even though I had met all of the Ds a couple of times at campaign workshops. I really don't remember when it happened, but I think it was in December that all of the newly elected legislators came to the Capitol for an orientation weekend. We didn't have parking passes or anything, and only the general working staff was present. ID pictures were taken, and we were given name tags and parking spaces.

Our first meeting was in the old Supreme Court room, and we met all of the party leaders from the House and the Senate. The Speaker and Minority Leader from the House addressed us. The Rs held a slim lead in the House. But there were co-leaders in the Senate. Democratic Senator Mike Gronstal was his usual charismatic self telling a few jokes. Stew Iverson was the Majority leader for the Rs. After the welcoming speeches from the leaders, we were given a detailed tour of the Capitol. What a magnificent building!

After viewing the cafeteria, elevators, law library, and a variety of other nooks and crannies, we became acquainted with the restrooms. Big item! The Capitol is big, but it has only one set of restrooms for visitors, and they are on the ground floor. There are some other special restrooms that may be used only by legislators and hired workers. We also learned the rules about bill writing and decorum. Did you know that Senators must wear a coat and tie while in the Senate chambers? The House Members can leave off the tie, but most wear both as well. Every Senator has his/her own clerk. This means that at each Senator's desk in the Chamber, there is a smaller desk for the clerk. There are also two chairs which are definitely different. Don't even think about sitting in the Senator's chair unless you are a Senator! Also, when the Senate is in order, only Senators may go up and down the center aisle. There are many rules in the Senate that are not adhered to by the House. Some Senators get more carried away with these than others.

I felt that all of the seven new Senators were looking forward to doing their work and making a positive difference for the State of Iowa and their respective constituents. We had one early meeting with Governor Tom Vilsack. We met in his office, and I remember him saying, "You guys can run this place if you want to." I didn't really understand that comment until after a couple years of learning the ropes of the legislature. Governor Vilsack was telling us that if we seven voted together on any issue, we could control the outcome of most. After two years, we had all been able to talk and work together on some different issues. We genuinely liked each other even though our approaches might be a tad different.

One night, we decided to go out to dinner together and talk about our viewpoints so far. We went to one of the many fine restaurants in Des Moines and had a great time. We sat around the table discussing reactions and our feelings about Gov. Vilsack's comment. We decided we wanted to come up with something that all of us could support and push through in a collective, bi-partisan manner without leadership interference. We discussed legalizing fireworks, a few other possibilities, and then settled on something in Education. Remember, three of the seven were educators, and four of us were former mayors. The subject of "social promotion" came up, and it was decided we had to develop something to provide schools with the backing to "hold back kids" when appropriate. Too many of us knew of situations where kids were being promoted to the next class without meeting the criteria. We had also listened to some of the education naysayers on how bad the public schools were and that we needed to do more in the area of testing and accountability. We wanted to promote and accentuate the positive.

Dave and I began working on a bill that would require that our K-5th graders read at grade level. If students fell behind, we would offer grant money that schools could apply for and use for initiatives to help improve reading skills. Students can't learn if they can't read! Reading must be learned in early elementary. We went on to address the Middle School children and did something similar in that we were going to require the passage of their core subjects (English, Math, Science, and Social Studies) or they would have to retake the failed classes. However, students would be able to move ahead. For example, they may be retaking 6th grade Math while moving ahead with 7th grade English, Science, and Social Studies. We would allow schools to apply for money for their initiatives. They could range from summer school, before and after school programs, Saturday school, or special tutoring.

Having been in the public school arena for over 35 years, I feel that the local schools have a good idea of what will or won't work in their district. I don't think there is a one-size-fits-all program that will address each individual school's needs.

All seven of us were on board and we got the bill written and submitted to the Education Committee. I remember running the bill in the sub-committee and passing it with very little problem. The only major problem was that we could only put $1 million into the bill. We had started with $5 M but had to cut back because the available funds weren't sufficient. I discussed the movement of this bill in the Power and Leadership chapters. Our Freshman bill was destined to pass but in a greatly revised version.

The "Super Seven" continued to have regular monthly suppers for the next two years. We became closer and worked together on many projects. It was amazing what we were able to solve when sitting around the table and working together using common sense. I think this is the way all of us had visualized how things would get done in the Senate when we were first elected. We said several times, why is it that we can solve things with what seems to be a good solution, but we can't get it done in our caucuses or in the Chambers? This, too, will be discussed (cussed) in other chapters. During our last two years, we seven continued to meet and discuss situations that were happening within our own caucuses. There was always friendship and respect.

One of the greatest things that came out of my first term was the relationship that I built with my fellow classmates. When I lost my reelection bid, the first two phone calls I received were from my Republican brothers. Having graduated from college and been in a fraternity, I feel that our class was more like a fraternity, and I am proud to be a part of this fine group. As my good friend Dave often said, "People are more important than things."

DAVE

How do you like change? Even though we may not always like change, it is inevitable. Being elected to the Iowa State Senate was a change I never anticipated. Let me explain . . .

A number of years ago I read a statement from some research that said "most of the people in the U.S. do not like their jobs." If this research was an accurate assessment, I have truly been blessed. I have been anyway, but in my more than 50 years of employment there was only one year where I wasn't excited each day about going to work. That year (1979-80) was my second year as Business Manager,

School Board Secretary, and Activities Director at the Sioux Center Community Schools. It had lots of good things, but I was looking for change. I really missed teaching and being involved with kids in the classroom. So when Northwestern College asked me to join the Business/Economics faculty, I couldn't wait.

My Dad was a painter and wallpaper hanger all of his working life. He loved it as his Dad had before him. But he told me not to follow in his footsteps. He died of a heart attack at the age of 56, and I was with him. The last words he said to me were "If you can't work, it's not worth it." That was at 2:35 in the morning of November 5, 1960. As you can tell, it strongly influenced my decision making.

Whenever I consider change, there are two other strong components for me. What does my wife Dot think about it, and what answers do we get from prayer? That's why I needed some time before I could tell those Sioux County party officials whether "we" (Dot and I) would run for that Senate spot. If Dot hadn't been willing to give up her "Parish Nurse" position with our church and go to Des Moines and be my Assistant, the issue would have been closed. But all of the answers came back "Yes," so we started the campaign and were fortunate enough to join that great Freshman Class of 2005. I still can't believe we were given the unparalleled opportunity to serve this great state in that fabulous building! My only regret is that I wish I had been younger and could have withstood a couple more terms. Yes, regardless of age or anything else, I would not have stayed more than 12 years.

Dot and I have so many fond memories of those four tremendous years with such a great cast of characters and friends. We are so thankful that those friendships continue to enhance our lives. May God continue to bless each of them.

Frank Wood Gallery

Presidential candidate Hillary Clinton visited us at the capitol during her '08 campaign. We discussed campaign issues.

(Top picture) Senator Mike Connelly from Dubuque retired after a long political career. I'm toasting him at a farewell party. (Lower picture) Here I am in Princeton, Iowa, walking alongside the Scott County Democratic Wagon.

When Joe Biden (now Vice-President) visited the capitol on his press run, I called Dave in for this photo op and a discussion about education.

One of the many perks was speaking with Hall of Famer and former Miami Dolphin Vern Den Herder and his wife Diane. Dave coached Vern as a high school basketball and baseball player.

One of the neat things Dave did was to sponsor a table at the Annual Easter Prayer Breakfast. He always invited our freshman group. Here we are with the main speaker, Tom Osborne, the Nebraska football coach. Names: L to R: Brad Zaun, Tom Hancock, Dave Mulder, Coach Osborne, Tom Rielly, Jeff Danielson, Frank Wood

Soon-to-be-President, Barak Obama made a campaign swing through my territory. It was my privilege to introduce him to 3000 people, with my son Brian present.

Four of the freshman class with Governor Chet Culver and Nancy Boettger at the annual Easter Breakfast. L to R: Tom Hancock, Frank Wood, Jeff Danielson, Dave Mulder, Governor Culver, Nancy Boettger.

"Leadership is the capacity and will to rally men and women to a common purpose and the character which inspires confidence."

Lord Montgomery

CHAPTER 7

Leadership Positions and Dealing with Lobbyists

DAVE

I don't think I could or would be a Party or Caucus leader. I've always been a leader in every other aspect of my life, but politics is different. First of all, there are some parts of it I hate. I hate to raise money, and this is a major responsibility of a political leader. I also don't like to be away from home so much, especially without my wife Dot. Party leaders must travel the state to meet donors and interview and recruit candidates for office. I could do it, but I wouldn't enjoy it.

Political parties and most candidates need lots of money. Many elections are now costing $400,000 to $500,000 per candidate. I think that's ridiculous, but it is reality. Television, radio, and newspaper ads, multiple mailings, yard signs, and mileage all cost a bundle. These are major negatives to me, but that's just a start.

Leaders set and control the legislative agenda. That is why parties want to be in the majority. They determine what bills will be written, what will be included in the bill, and whether the bill will ever make it out of committee and to the floor for debate. Leaders count votes and won't allow a bill to the floor unless they know it will pass. The party "Whip" does the counting.

Remember that in my first two years the Senate was split at 25/25. I recall a few bills failing during that time, but not many. It is not considered good leadership to bring up bills that fail to get a majority vote. In my last two years the Democrats held a 30 to 20 advantage.

Only one bill failed during that time, and I'll tell you that interesting story.

The Bill itself dealt with horses in some way, I don't remember exactly, but that's not important. The Senator floor-managing the Bill was a Democrat, a veterinarian, and a straight-shooter. In his presentation, he closed by saying the Bill was given to him by the Equestrian Group, was fairly non-controversial, and he wasn't convinced it was a vital piece of legislation. "So I think this is a free vote; go with what you think." We did, and the vote failed. Quickly, before the votes were locked in, the Democratic Majority Leader changed his vote so he could put in a Motion to Reconsider (M.T.R.)

Normally, each Bill that is going to be brought up on the floor is discussed in each party's caucus beforehand. Apparently that hadn't happened with this one, or a few Senators changed their minds during debate. Changing one's mind on how to vote is not real popular with the leaders. Suffice it to say that the next day, when the M.T.R was activated, the Bill passed handily. I think they did talk about it in caucus *that* time!

Don't get me wrong. Party Leadership is far from easy, and it is tenuous. Politics is hard, can be nasty, and keeping a leadership position depends almost entirely on how the party does at election time. In my four years I saw four different leaders of the Senate Republicans. The House Republicans also lost their majority status and replaced their leader. Win at the polls or lose your leadership position.

Another little tidbit that happened in my first year casts some reflective light. As an old coach I have experienced the necessity for teamwork if success is to be achieved. So in the Senate, what is the team? I believe it to be the entire Senate, not just the separate parties. All fifty Senators *should* work together to pass the best bills possible for the people of Iowa. That is not the belief of each individual Senator. Power is an important entity in many aspects of life. It is especially important in politics. Money can and does create power. Money is given to winners by lobbyists and constituents. Even with money and power, sometimes it is impossible for parties to reach agreement. When one party has a big majority, they really don't need the other party to complete their political agenda. They can "roll over" the minority, and this happens. Yes, it is done by BOTH parties.

Here are a few more quotes I heard in my first year. "The only time we need the minority is when we need a 2/3 vote." (This is needed for the Governor's appointees.) "Remember how they rolled over *us* when *they* were in the Majority!" This gives you a little of the flavor of what happens behind the scenes.

The 25/25 split hadn't happened since the 1960's. The parties actually needed each other and the leaders *had* to work together. At one of the receptions I happened to be in line with co-majority leader Mike Gronstal. As we visited I asked him how he liked the even split. He characteristically remarked, "I love it!"

Then I queried, "Would you like it to be like this all the time?"

"Oh no! That wouldn't be good. We have to have majority rule!" he exclaimed.

My final question was, "So when is the even split good?"

"Oh maybe every ten years or so."

End of discussion. Isn't politics intriguing?

Leadership comes down to influence. It is to the extent that we influence people that we lead them. Review Lord Montgomery's quote at the beginning of this chapter. All that I've discussed so far in this chapter is "stuff" I could deal with as a leader. I might not like it, would feel lots of stress, but could deal with it. I don't believe I could deal with what comes up in the next paragraph.

Lobbying groups give substantial sums of money to both parties and to incumbent candidates. Of course there are some groups that contribute more to one particular party than another. Examples: Iowa State Education Association (ISEA); Unions; Gay, Lesbian, Bisexual, Transgender, and Allied Union (GLBTU) almost exclusively support the Ds. Iowans for Tax Relief and Iowa Right to Life go with the Rs. Some groups pick favorites (whoever is in the majority) and others contribute to both because they don't want certain issues to ever be brought up. Why is it, do you suppose, that neither party could get a bill to the floor that would give another penny to the bottle and can redemption centers? The redemption centers in Iowa have been getting that same penny for over 30 years now. All of their costs of operating have gone up, but the revenue remains the same. Both parties have spent many years in the majority during those 30 years and neither could up the ante. Why may one smoke on Casino floors in Iowa, but virtually no other business places? Do you suppose money plays a role in those decisions?

I would really struggle with not bringing up some issues for debate because these issues were very unpopular or unwanted by groups that give strong financial support to the party, or to me.

Face it. There are many, many issues where the legislator knows much more about the cause and effects than does "Joe Public." You elected us to make many of those decisions for you, and you trust our judgement for the most part. That's good. That is what a "Representative form of Government" is all about. So after studying certain bills we can make better, more-educated decisions. Hopefully these will be best for our State. Voting is incredibly hard (at least it was for me!), but we have to do it to the best of our ability. If we do goof up, we can come back and try to remedy the situation in the next session. A good example of this is the "2000 foot rule" for sex offenders. It looked good, and we wanted to be tough on sex offenders. But it didn't work! Many law officers and other authorities working with the problem said it should be changed. The Legislators listened and in 2009 the rule was improved. That's the way it is supposed to work.

But there are many issues that were talked about, written about, argued in the back rooms, that never gave the people, who know just as much as we do, the opportunity to speak. What can it *possibly* hurt to have a statewide referendum on the Marriage Amendment? (Do you like it that Iowa is now known as the "Gay Marriage Capital" of the U.S.?) Why shouldn't the people of Iowa have an opportunity to vote on Term Limits? There are other issues that deserve floor debate at the least. But, more about that later.

FRANK

I was very excited when I was elected and found out there was a 25/25 tie in the Senate. To be honest, I truly didn't know what that meant. I just thought that it would be a great way to get both sides to work together and move things in a collaborative manner. I was all for that, and I felt that I had over 32 years experience with dealing with students, parents, and staff. I really felt that I was going to make a big difference. It was interesting to say the least.

Dave mentioned leadership, and the first couple of calls I received after my victory were from sitting Democratic Senators. They congratulated me but then asked for my support of them, as they sought leadership positions within the party caucus. I really didn't know too many of the other Senators except Senators Stewart, Courtney, and Gronstal. Senator Stewart was my mentor and someone who I called several times during my campaign.

Campaigning can be very grueling, frustrating, and downright unbearable. I was told that I was going to need to fund raise at least $150,000 to be successful in the election. I thought that was ridiculous. After my campaign was over, I had spent over $215,000! The amount of mailings, radio and television coverage, signs, etc. added up to a huge 450-vote win in 2004! My race was *not* the most expensive in the state. The race between Senator Zaun and the incumbent in the Des Moines area totaled over $900,000. Elections are won with *money*. Check it out and see just how many candidates won when they spent much less than their opponent. Don't forget to count the special-interest donors as well. You will see them running their own television ads, radio ads, and placing ads in the newspaper, and in targeted mailings against one of the candidates. Can you imagine spending over $500,000 in order to get a job that pays $22,700 (that's what it was at that time—now $25,000), for a part-time position?

I agree totally with Dave on being in a leadership position. One of the most undesirable things that a candidate must do for his or her election is to raise copious amounts of money. Without it, you can't get yard signs, send out mailings, advertise, get media coverage, or GET ELECTED!

DAVE

Many people have misconceptions about Lobbyists. I sure did! I think the relationship between Lobbyists and Legislators is different in Iowa than it is at the Federal level. I didn't know about or hear of any situations where "buying votes," "giving extravagant gifts or trips," or anything like that took place.

Iowa has a law stating that lobbying groups may not give anything worth more than $3 to any legislator unless it is offered to everyone in both parties. Remember all of those receptions referred to earlier? Since both parties are invited, the food and drinks may exceed the $3 limit. But if a lobbyist wanted to take me out to supper the most it could cost is $3. (Would you like half a Big Mac and a sip of Diet Coke?) I think this is a good law, and it seems to work well in Iowa.

Lobbyists are great sources of information. Of course they are biased for their clients. They are well paid and well informed on issues affecting their clients. And they had better help with favorable legislation and work well with legislators, or they won't have a job very long. There has to be mutual respect and confidence for good things to happen. I think I asked to talk to lobbyists about as often as they called me out to visit. Many times they just want to know where one stands on a Bill, or what information is needed. Oft times I asked the lobbyist, "Who doesn't like this Bill?" They always told me so I could visit and get both sides of the issue.

Another thing good about lobbyists is their willingness to try to find common ground. Legislators don't like to pass laws where there are definite winners and losers. We like win/win situations much better. (Duh!) Here's an example. Banks have some fundamental differences with Credit Unions. Both feel the other entity has some tax advantages. Legislators are not going to take sides here. When a Bill is presented and makes it to subcommittee, this is the time when Legislators, Lobbyists, and any other interested persons meet to discuss the Bill and make suggestions for change. If the Credit Unions and Banks are at odds on the wording or other issues, the Legislators will say "You two get together and present what you can agree on. No agreement—no passage."

I really enjoyed my relationship with the Lobby and appreciate how much they do to improve the Laws. I learned a lot from them. Did I agree with them all the time? Nope. But I tried to tell them why I believed the way I did and also tried to keep an open mind. That's not always easy for a stubborn Dutchman!

Since I'm talking about the Lobby, and the story you are about to read was told me there, I hope it tickles your funny bone the way it did mine. The Department of Natural Resources (DNR) person who told me, swears it was a sincere and legitimate call received in the DNR office.

As you are probably aware, Iowa has a great many deer, and they do cause some pain and consternation. They are the leading cause of accidents on our State's highways, so it is necessary to post many warning signs. As a result of these "Deer Crossing" signs, the DNR received this call. "I was wondering if you could move this sign somewhere else. We really don't like the deer to cross here, and besides, several of them have been killed!" You know? Even if it was phony, I love it!

Let me tell you a couple more positive anecdotes about lobbyists. I had received a call from a constituent about an Iowa law that was causing him a tax problem. He didn't think it was fair, and neither did I. He owned two small corporations that he wanted to merge into one. Both of the corporations owned a few motor vehicles. Iowa required that a sales tax be collected for the transfer of ownership of these vehicles from the one corporation to the other. As the constituent said to me, "I owned the vehicles in the morning, and I owned them in the evening. Even though no money has actually changed hands, now I have to pay sales tax on them again!"

Since we agreed that a change was in order, I requested the new bill from the "Bill Writer." (Iowa employs men and women who examine present laws and then write new bills to make the changes requested by legislators. They know all the codes and the jargon.)

The draft looked good to me so I talked to the Transportation Committee Chair, and some other key legislators to get the ball rolling. The Bill moved through sub-committee and then the full committee and was finally given to the floor manager. Since I didn't serve on Transportation all I could do was to encourage movement and then speak for the Bill's value, need, and rationale for passing when it got called up for floor debate. All of this happened and the day for debate arrived.

By the way, lobbyists always keep track of bills that affect them and let the legislators know of progress or the lack thereof. Just as the Bill was being called up, I received an urgent call to meet another lobbyist. I didn't recognize his name (this was my first year) but I went out to meet with him. He said, "Hey, you have a good bill here but there's a problem."

"What's that?" I asked.

"Well, you have the wrong code. Your Bill is dealing with the ownership of taxis! You need to change to this new code number, (he gave me the number). Just call for a short amendment delay and that will solve the problem."

This I thankfully did! That guy didn't know me from a bale of hay, but he knew his job and did it well. This whole business of passing laws may appear chaotic, and it sometimes is, but in my estimation it would be a whole lot worse without the lobbyists.

Here's another lobbyist story that has kind of an ironic twist. I had told my constituents that I would not vote to increase gambling in Iowa. This is a tough issue for me. I know the dangers of gambling, but I like to do it. Now, Now! Let me explain before you judge me too severely. I said I LIKE to gamble; it's exciting, fun, and dangerous. But limits are absolutely vital. Mine is a quarter. The Bible never mentions gambling in any negative way. In fact you won't be able to find the word anywhere in it. It does talk about casting lots ("the sacred dice") to settle issues, but I don't think that's the same. The last verse of Romans 14 does give me pause however. "If you do anything you believe is not right, you are sinning." Hmmm, do we all become great rationalizers and justifiers? I'm afraid I have, especially on this issue. So I do bet quarters on the outcome of games, golf matches etc. Since I keep track, I know I'm ahead over the years. If I ever get behind, I'll quit. There now, confession is good for the soul. That's not my only weakness by a long shot, but one with which I have to be very careful.

Now back to the story. A few years back in Iowa, it was legal for fraternal organizations, (Knights of Columbus, American Legion, and the like) to sponsor "Gambling nights." These would usually occur once a year and be money-raisers for the organization or for charity. But at some time the Legislature had passed a law outlawing these events.

I had a constituent (a member of the Knights of Columbus in a neighboring community) who wanted these events to be legal again. Since I looked at this as restoring something that had already been in place, and not an expansion, I agreed to help. This seemed like a justifiable reason to "gamble" if there ever is one. People attend and participate, hopefully with a financial limit, because they know it is "for a good cause." I can't tell you how much I've purchased over the years at church and college auctions (stuff I really didn't need, but was purchased "for a good cause"). I rationalized that these philosophies of a "gambling fun night" were about the same.

At any rate, this was a difficult law to get restored. If it hadn't been for the lobbyist cajoling, nurturing, and closely watching exactly how the amendment was being handled and being attached to a variety of bills, it never would have been passed. Well it did pass and you are now in the chair determining the goodness, badness, of the law—and me! (Another use of the website www.legis.state.ia.us is that you can find the lobbyists position on each bill being considered.)

FRANK

Because I was on the Education Committee, I had been selected to attend a National Conference of State Legislators (NSCL) in another state. Several of us legislators went out to eat together. A lobbyist offered to pick up the tab. I was with two other legislators from Iowa, and we all said in unison, "We'll pay for our own food." We then told the other legislators of our "$3.00 limit" and they all laughed. I can see how this could all get out of control. Would it be nice to go on a golf excursion? Sure would! But at what expense? A vote? I don't think that is what we were elected for.

I also found out that the lobby can do a lot for you. This is especially true when you are the Chairman of a committee or the floor-manager of a Bill. You find out rather quickly just which lobbyists are willing to work with you and which ones are not. Since I was in the majority party my last two years, I found myself floor-managing several Bills on the Senate floor. I had to work closely with the various lobbyists on each of these bills. If a bill was being moved by a certain group, I would meet with their lobbyist and find out first why we needed to run the bill. I would then ask who was against the bill and why.

At one point in my first year, I worked hard and long on a bill to get it passed. On the last day of the session, I found out that a colleague of mine in my own caucus made changes to that bill with amendments in the "Standings Bill" (A Catch-All Bill). Immediately after caucus, I found the lobbyists and told them about the changes. I found out later that they worked with the House members to get those changes out of the bill again. My colleague was upset enough that he left the chamber prior to the last vote of the night. My original bill remained the way I wanted it. The lobby can be, and is, a very powerful part of legislation.

"Politics is not an exact science."

Bismarck, 1863

CHAPTER 8

The Budget Process

FRANK

Have you ever wondered just how the Iowa State Budget actually comes to fruition? Did you know that the State has within it's own code that the spending budget is to be based on 99% of the estimated revenue for the coming year? Well that is the way it is, but that is also just the beginning.

Of course, one of the main problems is that everything in the proposed budget is based on estimations. There are also other uncertainties. What will inflation be? How about unemployment, weather disasters, union contract negotiations, and a myriad of other issues? We're talking somewhere in the neighborhood of $6 Billion that has to be allocated fairly and adequately in the areas of Education, Agriculture, Natural Resources, Economic Development, Health and Human Services, Justice, Transportation, Administration, and a few others. Every legislator has priorities, opinions, obligations, likes and dislikes to various parts of the Budget. The House, Senate, and Governor all have to reach ultimate agreement—and the budget has to balance. Sound like fun?

Well, it isn't. But it has to be done or we don't go home after either 100 or 110 days of negotiations. And by that time, we're all ready to go home. Remember, many of the legislators have other jobs waiting for them.

For my last two years, I was the Chairman of the Education Appropriations Committee. After receiving the targeted amount to be used by Education (60 to 65% of the total budget) my committee had to allocate funds to K-12, Community Colleges, Private Colleges,

Pre-School, and the Board of Regents. Appropriation Committees are somewhat unique in that they contain both House and Senate members. However, since the Ds held the majority in both the House and the Senate there was a proportionate majority of Ds on my committee as well. So whatever we decided, we were sure to be able to pass it. It was still important to me to reach out to the Rs for their input. That wasn't the case in all of the committees.

The Leaders and the Committee Chairs play a big role in the allocation of funds. Some funds have to be kept back to cover unexpected contingencies. Other funds are "borrowed" from other accounts to keep everything in balance. Both parties are guilty of "borrowing" from the various "Rainy Day" and Trust funds. Two of the biggest of these have been the Tobacco Settlement Fund and the Senior Citizen Trust Fund. These Funds were established for specific purposes (Tobacco for infrastructure, i.e. roads, sewers, bridges, etc. and Senior Citizens to provide funding for the elderly to be able to stay in their homes longer). Unfortunately, many times the funds were not replenished. Remember, BOTH parties have raided these various funds to give the appearance of a balanced budget.

The process is a long one and starts with the chamber (either the House or the Senate) that will take up the Appropriations Bill first. I had the pleasure of starting the process in my first year and then the next year taking what the House had completed and putting the final touches on it. I believe it is imperative to work across the aisle and keep communications open with your co-chair in the other chamber and with the Ranking member from the other party. Senator Nancy Boettger was my colleague on the Republican side. We already had established a good working relationship because she, along with Dave and Senator Brian Schoenjahn, had written the 4-year-old Pre-School Law in our first year. All of us were professional educators before coming to the Senate. It was also valuable that my co-author and I could discuss at length both sides of any issue objectively. I wanted all of the stakeholders to have an active voice in the direction we were going so as to get bi-partisan support on the final vote. There are very definite fundamental differences in certain funding ideas between the Rs and the Ds. Rs, in the years prior to my coming on board, kept low allowable growth percentages and passed several initiatives requiring more and more paper work by teachers and administrators. Some of this data work has provided valuable topics for educational discussions. I found it ironic, if not amusing, that some of these same legislators demanding portfolio collection, soon began to call it nothing more than scrapbooking.

As a teacher evaluator in both Iowa and Illinois during my career, I have found the portfolios to be a helpful tool with staff members and the evaluation process. The portfolio is great to show evidence of the need for improvement in certain areas of instruction. I can see where it could be labeled a scrapbook if administrators don't use it to bring about better instruction. I know it helped me to improve evaluation technique and provide motivation for each teacher to reach for higher learning goals. Many teachers have informed me that the way we used the portfolios has enabled them to improve instruction.

Now, back to the budget! The Education Appropriations Committee, besides the areas already mentioned, also provides funding for the State Library System, two special schools (Blind and Deaf), Non-Public Schools, Iowa Communications Network (ICN), and Public Television. It can be quite overwhelming when one considers how many employees, not to say all the kids, are directly influenced by the decisions we make. That kind of responsibility is stunning.

Governor Tom Vilsack had made it clear that he wanted teacher salaries in Iowa to move from 42nd in the nation to at least 25th. Teacher pay in Iowa had been much higher than it was presently, but over the years of low or no allowable growth, and many schools losing enrollment, the salaries by comparison had dipped to #42. Governor Vilsack announced an aggressive program of moving the teacher salaries back up to #25 or better in six years. In comes Governor Chet Culver, a former teacher, and he makes this improved salary situation an even bigger campaign issue. He wants to be 25th in three years by doubling the amount of money going into teacher salaries.

My first year as Chair of Ed. Approps. was a good one; the state had record revenues and we had ample funds to work with. We increased almost every line item. We also reinstated some of the programs hit by budget cuts in the years past and were even able to pass and fund the "freshman bill" that Dave and I helped write as freshmen, but with a much lower amount of money.

It is amazing that even with all of the open lines of communication, when the actual finalized bill came to the floor for debate there were a large number of amendments causing changes that would cost even more money. This "papering" ploy is often used by the minority party to cause those "bad votes" we talked about earlier. Every thing said in debate, amendments added and voted upon, will all be used later on the campaign trail. This didn't happen only on the Education Bill, but on all of the Appropriations Bills.

Remember the Standings Bill, the one that both Dave and I (and nearly all the other legislators) call the "Christmas Tree Bill"? That is the one bill that needs to be looked at with a fine tooth comb, because one will find quite a number of items requiring money for various special interest items. I found out that this bill was the major campaign issue used against me when I ran for reelection.

DAVE

Preparing the final budget is certainly not an exact science to say the least. It's probably the most important thing we legislators do down there, but it seems that efficiency is not a factor. I never served on the two biggies—Education or Health and Human Services. These two command around 80% of the total budget. I did serve my first two years on Administration and Regulation. It was enlightening, because that's where "Touch Play" was first introduced, but I was so "green" at what was going on, that I wasn't much of a contributor to establishing amounts for all of the functions. As is true for everything that happens in the Capitol, it was very educational and interesting.

I told you that voting was incredibly hard for me. Politics gets in the way too often. Writing your own bill is one thing, but working on other bills is another thing altogether. For example, I wrote (or helped write) bills on term limits, the cigarette tax, pre-school, commercial property tax changes, and many other amendments (that I first enlisted help on, from across the aisle) dealing with gambling, grandparents visitation rights, and many other issues I felt were important. I knew how I would vote on those issues.

But consider this from a politician's or party viewpoint. No one likes to be in the minority. Since it is the majority party that sets the agenda, many minority ideas (good or bad) will never get brought up or considered. Knowing this, the minority party can't be agreeable to what the majority party is doing or the people will keep electing them, keeping them in the majority. How do you think the Rs got the reputation of being the "party of NO"? The word is vote No for what the majority party wants to do.

Okay, here I am as a Republican working on what I consider to be my most important issue: Education. Frank asks for and receives my input. We work together to get what we consider is the best bill possible at this time. It is going to pass regardless of how I vote because the Ds have the majority. My party wants me to vote "No" because of the spending and the upcoming elections. Now before I tell you how I voted, here's another scenario.

Two of my best friends are grandparents. Their son's divorce, and the custody battle over the children, left them with no visitation or contact rights with their grandchildren. Being a granddad myself I wanted to do something. Iowa had passed a "Grandparent's Visitation Rights" law sometime earlier but portions of it had been declared unconstitutional, so grandparents had absolutely no power to do anything if one of the parents objected. So I worked with Jenny (a lawyer and a lobbyist) and she was tremendous help and became a great friend. Through her knowledge and guidance from a Supreme Court Lawyer we were able to get the "proper wording" to keep the Bill constitutional and still provide grandparents some opportunities for visitation and contact. It took a lot of work and a lot of time, but finally the bill was ready.

Because of politics again, we couldn't get it as a "stand alone" bill. It had to be attached to something for some reason. Where do we put it? Remember, the Ds are in power and nothing will get done if they don't approve. I enlisted the help of three other Senators from the other side of the aisle (Senators Keith Kreiman, Amanda Ragan, and Jack Hatch). All of them cared deeply about this issue as well. Jack was chairman of Health and Human Services Appropriations and he agreed to include the amendment on his bill.

There you have it. The two biggest "money bills" we will pass all year: One, Education and Two, Health and Human Services. How do I vote? Well, I voted for passage, and of course they passed. Many times I voted the 'wrong way,' I guess, but I don't think I'd do it any differently now. I'm sure I'm not the only legislator who felt or voted that way. I hope you have a little better understanding now of how the budgets are put together and how they ultimately reach fruition. Sound like fun?

"Politicians are like diapers; they must be changed often—and for the same reason."

Paul Harvey

CHAPTER 9

Term Limits

DAVE

I know that earlier I told you we would not try to convince you our position was the right one. Well, I changed my mind when writing this chapter! Sorry about that, but read on anyway, please.

I have always been a proponent of term limits. Numerous surveys show that the general populace also believes they are best. After serving four years in the Iowa Senate, I'm even more convinced that they are best for our state and country. But there are so many questions concerning the number of terms and the overall length that a person could serve, that many times the issue fails, or never gets brought up. See the Appendix (Legislative Information for All States) to see which states have term limits and the length of these limits. See also Number of Terms of Iowa's 83rd General Assembly 2009-2010.

For the most part, politicians do not like term limits. That should tell you something. There definitely are some negative aspects. It's a lot like mandatory retirement or early retirement. There are some people who remain very productive until they die of old age. Mandatory retirement is painful for them and for the place where they served. The same is true for some politicians. Some good ones would be out due to term limits, but, in my opinion, the gains would far outweigh the losses.

If a legislator knows he/she would be gone in, say, twelve years (the number I happen to favor), that person would sense some urgency and want to get at his/her agenda as soon as possible. This person might also be willing to work with others, regardless of party, to get these agenda items completed. I do believe limits are more important at the Federal level than either State or Local, but are needed none the less.

So much power and financial backing comes to the incumbent in any election. This, plus the name recognition that comes from longevity, makes it extremely difficult to defeat any incumbent in either a Primary or General election. I'll give you some Iowa statistics to support this statement in a bit.

This great country's Founding Fathers disdained lifelong politicians. Iowa in particular stated that she wanted a "Citizens part-time legislature." At the Federal level the only office where term limits are a factor is the President of the United States. George Washington believed two terms was adequate and he followed a self-imposed limit. (Do you suppose maybe old "G.W." would have been elected for a 3rd term if he had chosen to run?) Term limits were established after F.D.R. Think about this for a minute, since F.D.R., can you think of a President who had a "good" second term? Eisenhower, Johnson, Nixon, Reagan, Clinton, and George W. Bush are the ones to consider. As you consider each of them, do the following phrases recall some significance? U-2 incident. Sputnik. Vietnam War escalation and ultimate loss. Watergate. Sleaze Factor. Monica. 18% Approval Rating. Maybe we should elect a President for one 5-year term! Did someone mention "lame duck?"

So, why were term limits established after/because of F.D.R.? He was first elected in 1932 during the Great Depression. He was re-elected in 1936, and the Depression didn't start to end until the U.S. was pulled into World War II on December 7, 1941. By this time we had re-elected him again in 1940. We know it is hard to beat an incumbent anytime, but it is especially difficult when our country is threatened by or involved in a war. You may recall that Nazi Germany's Third Reich was very active militarily in the 1930's. If Roosevelt hadn't died in 1945, he would have completed at least 4 terms. By the way, Carter and George H. W. Bush are the only two incumbents defeated since Herbert Hoover.

Here are those Iowa incumbent election stats I promised. Since 1980, 84% of all incumbent Senators have been re-elected. It's even more lopsided in the House as 92% of the incumbent Representatives have been re-elected. In 2008, 26 Senatorial positions were up for election. Seven retired, 2 were defeated, and 17 won re-election. That's 84.5% for the incumbents. "How about the overhaul in 2010?" you say. That year, 21 incumbent Senators ran and 16 won, (76.2%). All Republican incumbents won. In the House there were 96 incumbents running and 12 lost (all Democrats). That's 87.5% so you can see that 2010 lowers the averages some.

See <u>Iowa Legislature</u> in the Appendix to see which party controlled the Governorship, Senate, and House in the years 1969/70 to the present.

Here is how the Iowa Legislature is organized.

50 Senators elected for 4-year terms.
100 Representatives elected for 2-year terms.

The annual Sessions begin in the first full week in January after January 1. It is a 100-calendar day Session in even numbered (election) years and a 110-day Session in odd numbered years. The salary is $25,000 paid annually to all legislators, plus an outstanding health insurance package. Each legislator is also paid $300 per month ($3600 annually) to cover expenses of supplies, postage, mileage, etc. throughout the remainder of the year.

This amount didn't even get close to actual expenses for me. But, in my opinion, this was the only item that wasn't more than adequate. For those legislators who have big geographical districts, (mine had three counties including 23 towns and a bunch of parades!) expenses run higher. My Representatives and I did over 50 public forums throughout the district each year. For non-rural legislators the amount may have been adequate. Each legislator is paid mileage for one round-trip to Des Moines each week of the Session. For the 100 or 110-days, Legislators are also paid a per diem (first year was $86, and the last year was $124; it is the same rate Federal Legislators are paid). Legislators are also paid a per diem and mileage during the interim when they take part in a party caucus, interim committee meetings, and conventions they may attend in other states. I don't believe money should be a motivator to run for office, and it must not be a deterrent, either. We need the best possible candidates running for office and representing us. It takes good people to write good laws. The leaders of each party, as well as the officers of both Houses, are paid additional stipends.

For the most part, party leaders, committee chairs, the Speaker of the House and President of the Senate all are experienced legislators. That's okay. Leaders have to earn the positions. How many years does it take to "learn the ropes" so to speak? There is a very steep learning curve in becoming a legislator. No one can possibly know everything about the myriad issues and bills that are presented. We averaged around 1500 bills each year and usually signed into law about 200. Each of us has areas of expertise. Personally, I thought my strengths would be in Education, Agriculture appreciation, Economics, Labor/Business, and maybe a little experience in dealing with people. I found there was still much for me to learn in each of these areas as well. But Judiciary, State and Local Government, Commerce, Appropriations, Human Resources, Rules and Administration, Natural Resources and Environment, Transportation, and Veterans Affairs kept me very humble. (Some of us have more reason to be humble than others!)

Although one has to keep learning with each year in office, (and I believe this is true in any occupation), there is no reason why one can't be effective in many ways the first year in office. I would hate to think I made no positive contributions in my first year. In fact, during an early caucus session one Senator indicated I might be a little too vocal on some issues. My retort was, "I have to be, I'm old and don't have much time!" I also think that if you can't get your priorities taken care of in twelve years, a replacement deserves a chance. Don't you think more will be accomplished when legislators are running out of time? Just think for example, about what is passed in the last few days of each session! Of course that can be a bit scary, too.

Because of the difficulty in defeating incumbents, many times it is difficult to find worthy candidates to run against them. Observe how many candidates "throw their hats into the ring" when the office is open and no incumbent is present. No one likes to lose. Everyone likes a level playing field. Incumbents have bigger financial war chests and ready access to party money and Political Action Committee (PAC) money. PAC's only give to incumbents, except on rare occasions.

Let's slip in another point at this juncture. I think Senate seats should be for six years (like the Federal level), and House seats for four (not like the Federal). Here's why. Term Limits of twelve years would be simpler and Iowans would save a lot of money because of fewer elections. We had some House and Senate races costing from $900 thousand to $1 M. in the 2004 and 2008 elections! Isn't it a bit ridiculous to be spending a half million to get a $25,000-a-year job? Why do you suppose that is? Could it be Power, Prestige, Love of Debt, or what? By changing the length of the terms we cut the number of elections in half and Representatives aren't constantly campaigning. Many politicians are reluctant to tackle anything controversial in an election year. Soooo, not much gets done. That's a significant consideration.

Since we're talking about saving money, here are some other considerations. Iowa now has 3 million people. This means each Senator represents 60,000 citizens and each Representative 30,000. There are twenty states having smaller populations than Iowa. Seven of these states have more Senators and eighteen have more Representatives. Look in the Appendix again at Legislative Information for All States to see the breakdown for each state on Population, Senators, Representatives, and length of Session. California is our most populous state with 36.5 million people. These are represented by forty Senators and eighty Representatives. So each Senator represents nearly a million people, and each Representative close to half a million. Are their people adequately represented? On the other hand, New Hampshire has only 1.3 million folks with 400 Representatives and only 24 Senators. So each Representative serves 3250 constituents and each Senator has 54,000! (I always believed Senators were more capable!) Of course the length and frequency of each Legislative session can play a role as well.

Think about these questions. Is non-partisanship getting better in Iowa and nationwide? Could this get better if term limits were applied? Is it worth a try? There are four states (Oregon, Massachusetts, Washington, and Wyoming) that have had a legal decision stating their Term Limits were unconstitutional. I don't understand this because our Presidency has had term limits since the late 1940's and fifteen states have approved them and had legal decisions indicating their legality. Two other states (Idaho and Utah) had their Legislatures vote term limits out again after eight years. (Remember, I think 8 years is too short and 12 would be better.)

When I proposed 4-year terms for the Iowa House, a long-term influential Senator said, "No other states do it." I'm not sure that is a good reason to do or not to do something anyway, just because nobody else is doing it. But of course there are other states (six to be exact) that do have 4-year terms for Representatives: Alabama, Louisiana, Maryland, Mississippi, North Dakota, and Nebraska. Remember that Nebraska has the Unicameral and has only Senators serving. Just for contrast, there are twelve states that have only 2-year terms in the Senate, and none have 6-year terms.

Another major argument against term limits is the statement made that "the politicians leave but the bureaucrats stay, and soon these unelected people run the state or country." If this is the case, it certainly shouldn't be! The elected official, even in his/her first year, is still the boss. Bureaucrats work *for* the Legislator and/or the party. So if we select candidates who are energetic, have principles, and a will to get things accomplished, we shouldn't have to worry about who is running the government.

It is going to take a ground swell of public opinion to fashion a change. Even then, there are no guarantees. When running against my predecessor, the subject of term limits came up. He stated, "When I campaigned for office I was for them. After serving 10 years, I've changed my mind." It seems the only way term limits can be passed is if all incumbents are "Grandfathered in" and not subject to the limits. Then, only the newly elected Legislators will be affected.

To accomplish the above change, it will be necessary to call for a state referendum because it is a change in the state's constitution. So rather than having the Legislature vote on whether Iowa would have term limits or not, the ultimate vote would be by the people. But the amendment has to be approved in two consecutive legislative sessions.

Regardless of where you stand on this issue (or any other for that matter) let your voice be heard. Ask the position of your Legislator on the issue, including the reasons why.

In summary, Term Limits save money, decrease power, remove incumbents, increase competition in several ways, and possibly promote more bipartisanship. I read a great article by Patrick Basham, a senior fellow at the Cato Institute. In the article, *Term Limits Lessons for Campaign Reform*, he substantiated a number of the points made in this chapter, and added a few others. He believes term limits "increase legislative diversity, decrease the centralized power of leaders, improve the quality of legislation, and foster smaller government." I've received his permission to include this article in the Appendix. Please read it and then decide for yourself if this is what we need. I had this article distributed to all of the Senate members, received several positive comments, but absolutely no action in committee!

FRANK

Dave and I discussed this at length a couple of times. I can see where term limits would serve a good purpose. But I can also see where they might be bad. At the state level, if you look around the capitol observing the legislators and their ages, you will see that a majority of them are older. When you take an even closer look at their years of service, those older legislators have a considerable number of years of service under their respective belts.

When I was elected, I was taken aback by the years of service and the ages of some of the Senators. There are a few legislators who are very knowledgeable and continue to work hard on providing great leadership to the citizens of this great state. Term limits will take some of the best out of the chambers and replace them with novices or less knowledgeable people. Who will be left to pick up the ball and carry it to the next goal?

While I was in the Legislature, I was still working as a building administrator (and still am), and I was able to be released from that job during my 100 or 110 days of session on a non-paid leave. I made sure that I talked with the more experienced Legislators to get a handle on how things worked in the Senate. That knowledge base is one of the things that I feel is needed to keep things in order and under control. However, I also see some Legislators who are not very productive, but they seem to continue to get elected term after term. So, one part of me believes that term limits can be good, but they can also be bad.

"We must always have old memories and young hopes."

Arsene Houssaye

CHAPTER 10

Some Perks and Great Memories

DAVE

Truly, there were 50 amazing elected men and women in the Iowa Senate! (Well, at least 49.) It was a pleasure to get to know them and work with them. There wasn't a day that Dot and I weren't in awe of where we were. "I can't believe I'm really supposed to be here," was a frequent comment as we walked into that magnificent structure. That feeling remained throughout our four years of service and continues to this day. What a privilege it is to serve the great people of Iowa.

This state has done a marvelous job of hiring personnel. The doormen in the Senate are excellent sources of wisdom, history, and love for our great state. It is an honor for me to call them friends. (Please look in the Appendix for the names of each of these gentlemen.) Dot and I were usually the third or fourth to arrive each morning. Being early risers, we got there about 7:00 each morning even though we didn't gavel in until approximately 8:45. Amanda Ragan, Joel Bolkum, Steve Warnstadt, and David Johnson were oft times ahead of us. This was a time to visit with the doormen and clerks. Jodi Grover, the clerk for Brian Schoenjahn, was stationed right next to us and always beat us to the Capitol. She's a special friend, lover of trivia (especially Presidential) and one of the proof readers of this book. I can thank Jodi for help with lots of things.

Mike Marshall, the Secretary of the Senate, is an excellent source of wisdom and decorum in the Senate. He also plays an integral part in the selection of the Pages each year. These young high school men and women are great and pleasant helpers to each of us. The ladies in the offices behind the Senate are indispensable. All of these people make us look good by doing yeoman duty. I never heard a complaint from any of them. They serve as great examples to all of us. (Please go to the Appendix to see the names of these great people.)

Senators need official certificates completed to be awarded to constituents for a myriad of accomplishments. Eagle Scouts, State Champions, Business Awards, 100th Birthdays, and lots of others need this special recognition. We also need well-written Bills, Amendments, Rules Interpretations, and Resolutions. All of these tasks are completed flawlessly by these great people behind the scenes. Jay Mosher is an old fella who controls the Bill Room. I think he's actually the first person to arrive in the morning because he gets all of the previous day's work ready for distribution. He organizes the Pages to help collate and distribute this bulk of material and then files each bill and law in "his room" so he can supply ANY individual Bill to any of us in a matter of seconds. No one envies his position but all of us admire what he does and the way he accomplishes this tedious job.

There are two gentlemen (now friends), Craig Cronbaugh and Bob Lamberti, who hold forth downstairs in the Legislative Information Office. Not only do they have great ideas for gifts and keepsakes, but they also are available, at the drop of a hat, to take pictures of us with Capitol visitors. They always have a smile and never appear "put out" when we call on them.

The "telephone ladies," computer whizzes, and those who serve in the lobby room are indispensable. Not only are all of these people courteous and friendly, but they do their jobs exceptionally well and are unforgettable friends. All of them make our memories of the Capitol most pleasant and they made us "look good" while we were serving.

One of the many reasons Iowa is a great state is our State Caucus system. (See discussion of how and why the system came about in Chapter Three.) Being the first in the nation during Presidential election years brings a tremendous amount of attention. Everyone running for President comes to visit us and campaign on numerous occasions. My favorite statement during the campaign summer of 2008 was, "I've had my picture taken with the next President!" The normal response was, "Who is it?" And my final retort, "I don't know, but I have a picture with him/her."

Every candidate came to the Capitol or to our Senate District. Since I'm an autographed-picture collector, the shutter box clicked for * Barak, Hillary, Mitt, 2 Johns, Fred, Mike, Rudy, Sam, Joe, and Alan, and even Newt stopped in. Meeting them all was exciting for me, and even though *they* don't know who they are in the picture with, I sure do. I've also met past-presidents George W. Bush and Bill Clinton. These are definite perks of the office, in my book.

* Obama, Clinton, Romney, McCain, Edwards, Thompson, Huckabee, Giuliani, Brownback, Biden, Keyes, Gingrich.

There are a few funny memories too. During the Session we get called out to the lobby quite often. If you're just a tad clumsy and in a hurry, that combination can cause rather eventful entries. There are four steps down from the main entrance to the Senate and the floor of the Rotunda. One day, in my haste, I caught my heel, missed the steps and slid unceremoniously to a stop on the Rotunda floor, flat on my belly. (Oh yes, I did rock a little bit.) This excited quite a few folks as an old grey-haired geezer hit the deck. Fortunately, the only thing hurt was my pride. Now it is laughable, but I didn't giggle much at the time. The concern of all the observers did make me feel better. Not good enough to ever want to do it again, however.

Legislators are invited to many breakfast and evening receptions throughout the Capitol and greater Des Moines. We did our best to attend all of them. At each one, the Legislator's name card is on a table and a name tag for the spouse is handmade at the time of arrival. My wife's given name is Dorthy, (yes, there's only one "o") but I have always called her "Dot." The companies sponsoring these receptions like people to be on a first name basis, so they print the first names in large, capital, bold print. The surnames are printed just below in smaller print. This particular reception occurred in our first year in Des Moines at one of the downtown hotels.

When Dot and I arrived, the name cards were prepared and distributed. **DOT** was printed boldly at the top and Mulder appeared below. We thought nothing of it at the time. I was called over to a particular gathering for a few minutes, and when I turned to find my wife, I saw her in a deep discussion with another lady. I could see it wasn't the most pleasant to begin with, and then they both broke out in laughter. Here's what happened. The lady came up to Dot and started complaining about some bridges in her home area that weren't getting proper attention and funding. Of course Dot was flabbergasted and had no idea what to say or do. When she said she really didn't have the vaguest idea what was going on the woman said, "Well why not, you're with the D.O.T. (Department of Transportation) aren't you?" as she pointed to her name tag. It didn't take too long to correct the misunderstanding and bring on the laughter. These two ladies continued a friendly relationship from that time on.

Did you know that everything that is said on the floor of the Senate is recorded? I didn't, much to my chagrin. In our first year, as we approached the end of the Session, we were experiencing a "late nighter." This is a peculiar difference between the Democrats and the Republicans. Many times the Democrats choose to debate many of the controversial issues at night. To be honest, I can't recall what the issue was on this occasion, but we were getting close to the bewitching hour and the debate didn't seem to be going anywhere. I pushed the "talk" button, and the President in the chair said, (rather reluctantly I might add) "The Chair recognizes the Senator from Sioux." Here was my response. "You know, I like country music. (This woke 'em up a bit.) There's a fella by the name of Bobby Bare who has a song." At that point I sang a couple bars of, "I wanna go home."

It got a few giggles, and ten minutes later we were adjourned. I had my fun but the surprise came Friday morning after returning home. When I would have a free morning I enjoyed going to my coffee group at the Dutch Mart in Orange City. (Still do for that matter.) This is close to my Northwestern College office. As I was crossing the highway a friend of mine (Virg Muilenburg) offered to give me a lift. I hopped in, and he said, "I can't believe it! This morning I wake up listening to you singing a country song on my radio." He didn't think it was that great. Needless to say I warbled no more in public.

Some other great memories include a variety of other celebrities who were brought to the Capitol. When the state helped support the building of the racetrack in Newton, famous race car driver and TV commentator Rusty Wallace was introduced. Dr. Norman Borlaug (World Food Prize) was honored. An Iowan, he is acclaimed for saving over a million lives because of his research. A great and humble man. Olympic Gold Metal winner Shawn Johnson has a great smile that disguises the tremendous competitive desire within her. Olympic champion wrestler and fabulous college coach Dan Gable made an appearance. Actor Tom Arnold was present at Gov. Chet Culver's inauguration. Pro basketballer and Iowa State grad. Fred Hoiberg (The "Mayor") was also with us. I'm glad he's now the head coach at his alma mater. It was a pleasure for me to meet these people.

One of the great privileges of being a Senator is the opportunity to honor individuals, teams, colleges, and other special groups on the floor of the Senate. Each year the Tulip Queens and their courts from Pella and Orange City make special entertaining and promotional appearances. These are great young ladies who represent these communities' special events very well. It was a pleasure to meet and host the Court from Orange City each year. Usually, I could get them in to see and be pictured with the Governor.

After being a Prof and Coach at Northwestern College for 25 years, it was always an enjoyable opportunity to pay tribute to this fine institution. Two Professors, Jeff Barker and Pete Koene, were selected as the Iowa Professor of the Year. Having two winners in the first three years is a great accomplishment, and it was my pleasure to have them featured at the Capitol and get pictures with the Governor. We also had a resolution to recognize Northwestern College and help celebrate her 150th birthday.

One disappointment came after Iowan Zach Johnson won the Masters Golf Tournament. The Senate wanted to pay tribute to Zach, but his schedule got so filled he couldn't make it. It was nice to meet his Dad and Mom, but I still want to meet the Champion. Resolutions aren't quite as much fun when the honoree isn't present.

Northwestern's Women's Basketball Team won the National Association of Intercollegiate Athletics (NAIA) National Championship in 2008, and we honored Coach Earl Woudstra and the team. The five starters were all seniors and, since I announced all of their home games, I knew them all. Debbie Remmerde (now Leusink) from Rock Valley, Iowa, was the most phenomenal shooter I've ever seen. I did honor her earlier for individual prowess. She did some things I never dreamed possible. Can you imagine making 162 3-pointers in a row? She actually made over 100 consecutively 5 different times. Yes, these were all in practice, but I've never heard of anyone else doing it. But Debbie is probably most well-known for making 133 free throws without a miss in game competition. That is the record for men and women at all levels of the sport: high school, college, and professional.

They even featured her on the CBS Morning Show. She was the NAIA Player of the Year twice and holds a great many school, conference, and NAIA records. Oh yes, she was an All-American scholastically as well with an A+ average.

Another memorable experience was honoring former Miami Dolphin great Vern Den Herder. Vern was an integral part of the famous "No Name" defense that played in 4 Super Bowls and won two of them. He was the starting defensive end on the 1972 perfect season team as they won every game including the Super Bowl. No other team has done this. Vern starred at defensive end for twelve years for the Dolphins. He was also inducted into the College Hall of Fame. Vern and his lovely wife Diane are from Sioux Center, where I had the privilege of coaching him in high school baseball and basketball. The NFL can use more men like Vern Den Herder. We all can.

People are much more important than things. I've always believed this, and that was one of the main things that made this job mostly fun. I told you the people in the Senate, and I mean all of them, are very special people. I intended to serve another term but changed my mind in the last couple of weeks of my 4th year. I will recount these decision-making happenings in the next chapter.

At the risk of being called a name-dropper, let me give you a thumbnail sketch of the special people that were a part of my four years in the Senate. Sen. Bill Frist, the majority leader at the time, spoke at a Republican rally in Des Moines. Sen. Sam Brownback (now the governor of Kansas) visited the Capitol as a Presidential candidate in 2008, and Sen. John Thune came to Sioux Center twice in support of John McCain. Frequent visitors were former Iowa Governors Robert Ray, Terry Branstad, and Tom Vilsack. The experience of these men provided wise counsel and a historical perspective that was valuable for all of us. Gov. Branstad served very well as President of Des Moines University, and then made another run for Governor, and won. Tom Vilsack moved on to be named Secretary of Agriculture by President Obama.

One real highlight was sitting at the same table with former Secretary of State Madeleine Albright. We discussed her book, and I later wrote her a letter about it. I received a hand-written note explaining her beliefs about the weapons of mass destruction in the possession of Sadam Hussein. She is a highly intelligent and fascinating lady. (I suppose you have noticed that I use "lady" much more than "woman." That is by design and a lesson I learned from my Mom. She said, "Any female can be a woman, but only the special ones are ladies." My Mom was a very special lady. Another special lady I had the opportunity to introduce to a rally in Sioux City was former First Lady Laura Bush.

Our neighboring states Governors, Mike Rounds from South Dakota, and Dave Hineman from Nebraska, attended a Conference with our Iowa Governor Tom Vilsack in Sioux City. They discussed current economic issues facing our states and answered questions from the audience. All of our neighboring states should work more cooperatively with each other. Too many times we find ourselves in conflict with each other as opposed to working together for the betterment of our citizenry. Tax Structure, smoking bans, gambling laws, and speed limits are just a few areas where conflict supersedes cooperation, in my opinion. I'm sure you can think of other areas where this is the case. Competition, one of the Cornerstones of Capitalism* (see the Appendix) is supposed to produce a better product, for less money, and bring the best out of people. How many times do you see it doing just the opposite by bringing out the worst in us?

Radio and T.V. commentators Fred Barnes and Juan Williams were featured guests at a regional summer convention that I attended in Michigan. It was most educational to listen to these men during their presentations and then to visit individually with them later. They possess amazing insight as to what is happening inside the Washington D.C. beltway.

It was also a great privilege to meet Congressional Medal of Honor recipient Col. Bud Day in Sioux City, as we honored the great men and women who serve in our military.

Another special privilege was serving on the Iowa Prayer Breakfast Committee. This annual breakfast is held the Thursday before Easter (Maundy Thursday) and is always worth attending. I had attended a few of these special events before being elected so I was particularly gratified to serve on this committee. It was exciting for me to get two of my friends to come in as speakers: long-time Executive Secretary of the Iowa High School Athletic Association, Bernie Saggau, and the all-time great Nebraska football coach, Tom Osborne. These two men are not only great and inspiring speakers, but also outstanding Christian gentlemen. Another speaker of note at this breakfast was

Evelyn Husband. She is an author and the wife of astronaut Rick, who was tragically killed in the crash of the space ship Columbia.

All of these notables made my life more exciting, and it was certainly a pleasure to be with them. I know I met all of them, but except for Tom and Bernie, they won't have the vaguest recollection of meeting me. That's okay too.

Serving in the Iowa Senate is a tremendous privilege. One of the neat things that happen when one retires is the tradition of honoring each retiree with a Resolution. At this time other Senators rise and say nice things about you. This happened to me and it brought many tears to my eyes. One of my regrets is that my best friend in the Senate, Frank Wood, didn't experience this. Unfortunately, he was defeated in the next election. Had I had the opportunity, here's what I would have said:

"Frank, thanks for being such a good friend. It was great to work with you here in the Senate, especially on Education, but even better on a personal and family level all year long. You are always level-headed, calm, and reasonable. These are great qualities. I can readily see why you are also a great administrator. Thanks, too, for always being honest and forthright with me and other members of my party as we tried to work together. I can think of numerous times where you went out of your way to set some of my constituents' minds at ease. To me, you exemplify the kind of person I would want representing me. Would you consider becoming a Republican again?

Thanks for great service my friend, and may our God continue to bless you and your family."

FRANK

There really were some very special benefits and perks when you become an Iowa Senator. Dave mentioned the numerous interactions with potential Presidential candidates. I too, had my picture taken with several of them, both Republican and Democrat. Dave and I, along with fellow freshman Senator Brad Zaun, made a pact to get each other when one of the candidates came to the Capitol.

One of those memorable moments was when Mitt Romney visited. Brad and Dave had both publicly endorsed him, so when he came they quickly got me to join the gathering. "C'mon Frank, we've got to hustle to the second floor and meet Mitt!" We rushed out of the chambers and down the stairs to the hallway close to the Governor's office. As I got closer I starting walking a little slower because of all the lights and television cameras. I could see Mitt was holding a press conference, and there were a number of elected Republican legislators grouped behind him. Brad and Dave quickly joined the crowd, but I hung back and actually stopped and even put my hand over my face, just in case a picture was taken and I could be identified as a participant in the crowd. How would that look to my Democrat constituents? I felt out of place, but I really wanted to meet this man who might become the next President of the United States.

The press conference ended, and both Brad and Dave took Mitt by the arm and walked him directly back to me. I was standing on the stairway leading up to the back side of the Senate chambers. I was honored to meet such an individual, and I wished him the best of luck and told him how much I admired working with both Dave and Brad. I remember hearing a bunch of clicking sounds around me when I was talking to Governor Romney. There were a slew of media cameras taking pictures of my discussion. Our little visit only took a couple minutes, as was true with all of the candidates' visits. These people are incredibly busy.

As I walked back up the stairs I heard one person say, "Who is this Senator Wood?" The response was, "He's a Democrat." I thought, "Oh, no! That'll be a media caption!"

The very next day, I picked up the morning Des Moines Register, and right on the front page was Mitt Romney's picture during his press conference. Just over his right shoulder, way back in the crowd, on the stairs leading to the Senate chambers, is a fellow I recognized very quickly. Oh Lord! Was I going to get some rebuttal from my caucus as to just what was I doing there? I wasn't quite sure, but I knew it was harmless, so I wasn't really worried. Dave and I had a good chuckle over all of this.

I also tried to go to all of the receptions and legislative breakfasts I possibly could. There were many weeks when I didn't have to buy any breakfasts or suppers because of the numerous invitations. Of course, it wasn't a great healthy diet, and there was usually an abundance of alcoholic beverages available to those who cared to imbibe. After the first year and attending as many receptions as I did, I figured out which ones were most beneficial. Who had the best food and beverages, and which were the most educational and political.

The best perks to me were invitations to travel across the U.S. and be a part of several State legislative functions. Two major legislative groups work to arrange these informative gatherings: National Council for State Legislators (NCSL) and Council for State Government (CSG). These two organizations enabled me to travel to several spots throughout this great nation. I was able to travel to San Francisco and tour a drug company's lab and get a better understanding about drug production. I also traveled to Phoenix, Tucson, Dallas, Hutchinson Island, Washington, D.C., Hilton Head, Wilmington, and Chicago. Some of the responsibilities involved being a panel participant for the Before and After School Alliance as well as being involved with research in the field of Education.

I only regret not having the chance to have my friend Senator Mulder along with me during several of these educational seminars. I remember sitting in a small group with a researcher from Harvard discussing the advantages of early childhood education. He spent over an hour and a half with our Iowa group, which consisted of two Republican senators, the Governor's education aide, the Democratic senate education staffer, and me. After we heard the Harvard Professor's positive research, he had to leave. We Iowans continued our discussion concerning the importance of early childhood education. The Republican senator who was the co-chair of our Education Committee ended the meeting with the following comment: "I don't believe his research." I was flabbergasted and couldn't believe what I just heard. The senator had asked no questions of the professor during the hour and a half—nothing! We did have a discussion concerning 4-year-old costs and being able to do the education in kindergarten.

I strongly feel that the earlier we can begin teaching our youth, the more beneficial it will be for our country and state. We still have a huge gap in the readiness of our young people. This disparity causes many problems for our teachers being able to spend the necessary time with each student to give him/her the beginning and the foundation that each needs to be successful. This topic can be debated as well.

I know that Senator Mulder and I could agree with the outcomes that we wanted with regard to educating our youth. But we did have differing ideas on *how* to reach these goals. One thing was certain: we both had the best interest of each student at hand. Ultimately, Dave, Nancy Boettger, Brian Schoenjahn, and I, (all Senators and professional educators) wrote the initial Bill that became the Early Childhood Education plan for Iowa. Two Republicans and two Democrats with a common goal got the job done.

Dave mentioned the number of bills and the vast amount of information that is shared at the Capitol. I know of no one person who is an expert in all of the fields and areas. However, among the 50 senators and the staff members who help them, you can find someone who has expertise in any field. The amount of experience, knowledge, and research available on any given subject is more than ample to find solutions.

During my four years in the Iowa State Senate, I was able to wish several Senators adieu and yes, I stood and wished several colleagues, both Republican and Democrat, the best of luck. The hardest one to say good-bye to was Dave. He was by far my closest friend in the legislature and still remains a close comrade. We share one week during the year, vacationing in Myrtle Beach with our sons, competing in the National Father/Son Golf Tournament. It's one of the highlights of any year. It is something that we both look forward to, and it has brought me that much closer to Dave. I know our cell phones have each other on speed dial!

"Commit your work to the Lord, and then your plans will succeed."

Solomon (Proverbs 16:3)

CHAPTER 11

The Finale

DAVE

Well, here we are approaching the end of this book. There are a few loose ends to tie up and then we'll glance at the future.

Politics is definitely about communications. *How* we communicate with each other is just as important as *what* we are trying to communicate. Many times I saw bills and amendments killed because the senator who presented them was disliked. Conversely, numerous bills and amendments were moved along because the floor manager was well-liked. I guess that's human nature, but it's also too bad. Good ideas and good legislation die, not because of their merits, but because of the demerits of the presenter.

It seems that senators have long memories. They also seem to remember the negatives longer and better than some positives. Maybe this fact is another validation for term limits. Oft times, I heard about an incident that had happened many years previously, and that was why cooperation could not be present now.

Name calling, shaming, and a lack of tact will do nothing but divide and separate. It's not our place or intention to name names in this book. What good would that do? It would be counter-productive.

Some bills presented by unpopular senators are immediately placed in the "kill drawer" of the committee chairperson. This means they will never be brought up for discussion or assigned to a sub-committee. The "kill drawer" is also used for certain controversial issues that are not on the majority party's agenda. This is important information for any of you intending to run for office, or if you are unfortunate enough to be represented by an ineffective communicator. Suffice it to say that there were members on both sides of the aisle, who, when they rose to speak, did not ever win over even one opponent.

Remember, this is my perception. Do I honestly believe this is the way it is? Yes. Could I be mistaken? Yes again. I have shared these views with other legislators, and they have concurred. Think—Question—Research—Ask—Experiment—Evaluate—Adjust. These are all things each of us must do as we make decisions on what is happening.

Remember what that great New York Yankee philosopher Yogi Berra once said, "You can see a lot just by watching." Sage advice when it comes to politics.

Gentleness should never be confused with weakness. But a gentle non-accusing rebuttal or comment will, more often than not, win the day. A failure to show that gentleness can be a sign of immaturity. The same consideration and respect one shows within a family or in a business place is much needed. Politicians know that everything is recorded and that the press is always present. This fact alone should cause everyone to maintain composure and choose words thoughtfully. This wasn't always evident.

So why did I retire after only one term when I had publicly announced a couple months earlier that a second term was part of the plan?

As the old advertisement for Anacin used to say, "It takes a combination of ingredients," and I'm not sure which ingredient was the most important one in my decision.

First of all, I've always been very aware of my own mortality. The male members of my branch of the Mulder family all died relatively young. Heart problems were the culprit. Both of my granddads died at 62. My Dad was 56, and his three brothers died at 38, 49, and 57. All had heart attacks. All of them smoked and three of them got quite heavy. So athletics and the knowledge that life can be cut short or altered by smoking and extra pounds strongly influenced my life style. I knew smoking and drinking were not only detrimental to my being a good athlete, but also deterrents to a longer life. So they have never been a part of my life. As a coach and politician, I did my best to curtail their usage at any time.

Stress gave me a lot of grief during my coaching career, and I was seeing those same symptoms dominate my life again. Gaining weight, poor sleeping habits, and anger were increasingly evident. I don't get angry at or with people very often (trying to fix things with tools is another story). In the spring of 2008 all of these things were happening more and more frequently. My weight ballooned 30 pounds to 240. And it wasn't muscle. I contracted a case of shingles, even though I had had the shot. Temper and frustration seemed to be a part of each day. To be totally honest, I expected to have struggles with the "other" party on some issues and maybe with some constituents, but I didn't expect it so much in my own party. That came to full fruition one night when we were debating the Iowa Smoking Ban. Before I relate that story, here's a little personal background.

I have been a fortunate man throughout my life. I married the gal of my dreams, have two great kids and two grandchildren. Our kids have married well, and that's another blessing. I have absolutely loved my teaching and coaching jobs in high school and college. But I had always said that I would retire at 65. First of all, I never thought I'd make it to that age, and secondly, I thought that if I did, it was necessary to get out of the way and make room for younger people. Surprisingly, I made it to 65 and retired from Northwestern College. But I didn't want to! I wasn't ready to be "put out to pasture." That's why, when asked, I was ready to try politics. I'm so glad we did.

My wife Dot and I had carried out a plan so that we would be debt free by the time I reached 62. We reached that goal and money was/is not a problem. But people have to feel needed, useful, and stimulated to action. Being in the Senate surely did all of that, and then some. I loved 85 to 90% of it. But the 10 or 15% I didn't like, I really didn't like. My idealistic nature conflicted greatly with the realistic side. I'm also not a very good compromiser. Especially on moral, social, and Biblical issues. (What's that they say about stubborn Dutchmen? "You can tell them, but you can't tell them much.")

Several people told my wife that I was "too honest" and "too nice" to be a politician. First of all I don't know that to be true, but just the thought that some people think honesty and niceness don't jibe with politics is a very sad commentary.

You already know how I feel about smoking. I battled that issue time and again in my own caucus because I had campaigned for the dollar per pack tax increase. I also believe laws should be as fair as possible for those involved. That was the problem for me with the Smoking Ban Bill.

The Bill started in the House. In my estimation it was a lousy bill. It had exemptions, unfairness, and some items nearly impossible to adjudicate. Here are some of the objectionable things, in my opinion.

First of all, it exempted casinos, bars, and anything military. In other words, one could smoke in a bar operated by the American Legion, but not in one owned by a private citizen. It also banned smoking on any incorporated farm and other commercial businesses. The businesses, restaurants, schools, and public properties were fine with me, but not the incorporated farms. For those families who incorporated their farms it meant they could not smoke on their own land or on any machinery and equipment. Other farmers, who had not incorporated their farms, could. Also, one was not permitted to smoke within ten feet of a non-smoking facility or property. Think about that for a minute. You walk by a legal bar smoking and there is no penalty, but you go a few steps further and now you're next to a café or grocery store, and you have broken the law. Do the police have to watch for this? Nope. Citizens do. Do they report it to the police? Nope again. The Dept. of Human Services is responsible. The fine for the smoker is half of the fine for the business place. Both amounts go up on the second and third offences. This Bill had some other problems, but I think you get the idea.

This Bill had passed the House and was going to be brought up in the Senate. Remember, Bills don't get called up unless they have the votes to pass. So it was going to pass unless we could make some changes. The Republicans wouldn't vote for it, but they wanted it to pass because we could reap voter benefits at the next election. There were some Ds who wanted some changes as well, so the final content was somewhat in doubt.

The Democrat Senator floor-managing the Bill came to me and asked what it would take for me to vote for the Bill. I said, "It will have to be cleaned up by not exempting casinos and bars, and get that incorporated farms and ten-foot rule out." She said, "If I can do that will you be the 26th vote?" I said I would. Would you believe that she got it done? She did.

Now my Republican caucus had a problem. They didn't want any Rs to vote for it. The Ds had 25 votes and needed one more. When I said I had promised to vote for it the pressure began. I was told I didn't have to keep that promise because the Veterans Home in Marshalltown and the State Prisons were still going to be exempted. To be honest, that didn't concern me. Those weren't being exempted for money reasons like casinos and bars were. Nobody was going to the retired vets' home or to prison so they could smoke. After a while I got more and more angry and said, "I'll disappear and wait until the votes are in. If the Ds can come up with 26, it's a non-issue. Otherwise I will keep my promise and vote for it. But I've had enough, and you won't have to worry about me any more because I'm not running again."

I walked out. Eventually the Bill was brought up. I spoke on the floor about my beliefs and when the voting started I left the floor. Let me add at this point that there was one fellow Republican Senator who told me as I left caucus that he was going to wait to vote and then vote the same as I did. I already had tremendous respect for this gentleman and it continues to grow.

When I returned to the floor the vote stood at 25 to 23. My vote and my friend's weren't registered. I pushed the "Yes" button, so did he, two other Rs switched their votes, and the Bill passed 29 to 21.

Since the Senate passed a different Bill than the House, a Joint Committee had to be formed to write the compromise Bill. This was done, and the gambling floors of casinos were again exempted. So were the Vets Home in Marshalltown, the Prisons, and the State Fairgrounds. I didn't vote for the final Smoking Ban Bill because of the exemptions. It passed on a party-line vote, 30 to 20.

Am I sorry about the decision? Do I miss the Senate and the political world? No, I'm not sorry about leaving; it was the right thing for me to do. I lost the 30 pounds. I'm sleeping better, and my stress level is much lower. But I do miss the people. I also miss the excitement, the issues, and the Capitol. If I had been younger, I would have continued the battle. It needs to be done. We must work together to make Iowa an even better state. Jim Valvano, the late great coach of North Carolina State said, "Never give up." He's right. We must stay involved and informed. Always vote. Run for public office. Serve others. Our country and our great state need great people working and serving.

As this book draws to a close, here are some final thoughts for you to think about and act upon. Government is a necessity, but it is not (and never has been) an efficient, well-oiled machine. Remember the "Cornerstones of Capitalism?" Particularly the Profit Motive. No government at any level HAS to make a profit. And they don't. That's why we have a 17 Trillion Dollar National Debt in our 236-year history. Actually, in 1836 the U.S. had no national debt, so we have established over 17 Trillion in debt in 176 years. Congress is run by committees. Committees are not very efficient either, and they are not all focused on what is best for America, our State, or sometimes, our community. Government is most efficient and effective at the local levels. Committees can be controlled by individuals more concerned with individual power and reelection and not by what is ultimately best for the majority. Many times compromise is necessary, but it oft times does not produce the best product. The best product doesn't include "pork." (Pork: unnecessary additions to bills (earmarks) that are wants not needs.)

Congress will take care of itself first. Why do you think our Federal Representatives and Senators are not part of the Social Security system? Because their plan is solvent and better. Even our 150 Iowa legislators have a "Cadillac" health insurance package and a "pretty fair country" part-time pay package. At least it was the best I'd ever had in my 45-year education career.

This is why I believe we need people who are sacrificing themselves for the betterment of the whole. Being elected to the office is not the final goal: serving is. I know this is idealistic. Did I always act this way? Unfortunately, no. That was my goal, but I didn't always reach it.

The motto on our money says, "E Pluribus Unum." "Out of Many, We Are One." It's amazing what one person can do when he/she is focused, unselfish, and loving. Who are your heroes? Why did you select them? There's only been one perfect person to walk this earth, and we crucified Him. We aren't perfect, and we can only do our best. That's what each of us must try to do. Without a doubt, our great nation and our great state have some problems. But they are not without solutions. Each of you can have a positive impact. We need that.

Our money also says, "In God We Trust." He is the only One it is always safe to trust completely. Life isn't easy, but it's sure great to be in America. May our Lord bless each of you.

P.S. On the last page of the Appendix we have enumerated several laws Iowa needs, in our opinion. Give 'em a look and let's get the ball rolling.

FRANK

Well, the finale is upon us, and I have a chance to reflect on my one term as a State Senator as well as my unsuccessful run for re-election. I hope that while you read this book, you were able to see that Dave and I had several agreeable times throughout our term in office. We discussed many issues at length and did disagree on some, but we respected each other's views. I'm more of a Chicago Cubs fan than a St. Louis Cardinals fan. Does that make me more used to losing? I don't think so!

When I made the decision to get involved in politics and ran for Mayor of Eldridge, I ran on a simple platform that I felt enabled me to do a better job than was presently being done. I wanted to bring people together to discuss issues and hopefully make things better for the people of our city. In the three short years that I was in office, I felt we were able to do that, as well as to set up a plan enabling others to participate in a "strategic plan." That plan took a great deal of time to organize and involved over 100 citizens from Eldridge. I felt that the small amount of money that was needed to put it in place was well spent. It brought influential and knowledgeable people together to discuss ideas, formulate plans, and come to an agreement as to what directions we should pursue. I didn't feel that it was my direction, but rather the direction of the people that made this a successful plan. It was interesting to listen to people in our community presenting and discussing many things that previously I had never considered important. But they were important! At the meetings, we all had the chance to be heard, and that produced good feelings. As a result, we came up with an agreed-to plan that produced willing workers and advocates.

After being approached to run for the Senate, I took along that same attitude of listening, cooperating, and working together for common goals. At party meetings, party leaders gave me much information about the best ways to campaign. The importance of "door knocking," putting together an effective "stump speech," and doing the dreaded fund-raising were all covered. The amount of money needed to run a campaign has become outrageous. I have given a lot of thought to campaign reform and even considered state-funded campaigns. Limiting the amount of money to each candidate should make it more equitable for more people to get involved. Have you seen the "war chests" that some of our federal and even some state candidates have at their disposal? We're talking millions and millions of dollars.

My first campaign ran over $225,000, and my re-election bid was much the same. I have to say that raising money for the second term was easier than the first. Donors are a little skeptical when a candidate is taking on an incumbent, largely because incumbents have an 80 to 90 percent success rate. This rate was a little lower in the fall of 2010 because of voters' overwhelming dissatisfaction with the past. People have not been happy when all three branches are controlled by just one party, regardless of whether it's the Ds or the Rs.

Dave and I have tried to show the several things that come into play when making laws. A large majority of the time, at least at the state level, both sides have come together and worked to make better policy, whichever party is in the majority. I also feel that a large majority of the legislators at the state level seek office in order to make things better for their constituents. However, party politics does get in the way from time to time. You may also have noted that within each party, disagreements exist as well. Dave alluded to this concerning the Smoking Ban. He also mentioned that some said he was too nice and too honest to be a politician. I felt that he was a great politician, but he struggled with the party politics. I struggled with it as well, and I know that several of my colleagues did also.

Now back to my re-election bid. I must confess that I was not 110% into this campaign thing. I had difficulty finding time to do the things that needed to be done the way I had done them the first time around. I was given a full-time campaign manager. She was a young woman from the Des Moines area who had a little background in running campaigns. She was very nice to have around and was very helpful. At this time I had a different job at the high school. As Activities Director my job didn't allow for me to have as much time away from school in the evenings and during school-time, as I had had in 2004. I couldn't man the phones on a regular basis, and the time for knocking on doors was left mainly to Sundays and seldom on week days. My committee members also felt that I didn't have much to worry about in my bid for reelection. Therefore, because of my schedule and their overconfidence, I fell behind in the general campaigning. I believed that I would still come out on top, but the polling updates indicated it was an extremely close race. I remember those same polls during my first campaign. As a challenger, I just went out and worked all the harder when the numbers weren't so positive. Both races went down to the wire. I won the first by a "whopping" 450 votes, but lost my reelection by 351. So close!

Two days after the vote was counted, we received word that my wife Peggy had breast cancer. I felt like I had just been hit with a one-two punch—first my re-election defeat, and then my wife with a potentially life-threatening illness. I know that I have been down before, but I am not sure I ever felt that low. I have always said that God works in mysterious ways. I think He was making sure that I was around to help my wife during this particular time of need. It was a comforting feeling to know that I would be by her side during the next months. We have received good reports from the doctors for the past months, and we feel pleased to have had some of the most caring physicians and nurses making our journey much easier.

Many people have encouraged me to jump into some other political races, and many have said to give the Senate another try. They have indicated they would work much harder for me this next time. When I received a call from Chris Gallin, County Board Supervisor, and she encouraged me to run for her vacated seat, I took a strong look at that position. I decided to "throw my hat into the ring." After that, six Republicans and three other Democrats joined in the race as well. (See how many people are interested when the incumbent isn't running?) So I decided to continue to politic and I hope to be a public servant once more.

I am still being prodded into running again for the State Senate, or even better yet, Iowa Congress or Governor. It is a humbling experience that some people have the confidence in me to even think about those high positions. I am not inclined to look at the higher platform unless there are major changes made in overall campaign reform, less partisanship in the law making, and fewer personal attacks made on the candidates to discredit their image, family and values. I have seen these attacks become more and more personal, more demeaning, and, in most cases, based only on snippets taken out of context. I understand the meaning of freedom of speech, but with the many special interest groups, and the amount of money that is spent on these attacks, I wonder just what better things this money could be used for. There are many needs in our local communities throughout this great state.

This may sound like "sour grapes," but it is not intended to be. I would just caution each and every one of you to really take a close look at all of the candidates, ask pertinent questions, and ask yourself which candidate truly represents what you stand for and has the best chance to improve our government. I enjoyed my four years in the State Senate and, maybe at some future time, I may take another crack at that seat. I still feel that I have something to offer, and as long as I have that feeling, I will continue to seek some sort of public position.

"Where Senators shall mingle tears with smiles . . ."

Shakespeare

CHAPTER 12

The Last Word

DAVE

As was mentioned earlier in this book, we learned a lot in those four years in the Iowa Senate. In June of 2012, we asked, has anything changed in these last four years? If possible, it appears that it has become even more partisan. That's too bad, because very little positive gets done when there is no cooperation.

Remember, the Governor and the House is Republican and the Senate is narrowly Democrat (26 to 24). In each of these Sessions, both parties talked about Commercial Property Tax Cuts; Job Creation; Improving Iowa's Educational Status; and finding the Proverbial "Common Ground." Apparently none could be found because nothing substantive was passed in any of these areas, in spite of the fact that legislators went well past the ending deadline each year. In fact, one year (2011) the Session was extended to the last day in June when it was supposed to end in April! The cause, in my estimation, was once again the overuse of Power and the increasing need for Term Limits.

The House passed many Bills, many of which were never even brought up in the Senate. The Senate passed far fewer Bills, and a goodly amount of those were not acted upon in the House. A classic example of gridlock. There was a great deal of "posturing" by both parties in order to try to enhance public opinion for the upcoming elections. Inefficiency in politics is very expensive. Even though the legislators no longer receive their per diem (now $132) after the 100 or 110 day limit is reached, it still costs the taxpayers nearly $50,000 per day to keep all of the functions of government operating at the Capitol.

I mentioned previously that economists must "Describe, Explain, and Predict" in order to be viable. When I thought this book was going to be published in 2008 I predicted that the Democrats would have a substantial victory whether Obama or Hillary was the candidate. I also thought the "coattails" would be long, sweeping many Ds into office and allowing them to control both the House and the Senate in Iowa and the nation. The reason of course, was the economy and the fact that when the Rs controlled all three Branches at the Federal level, we didn't "act like Republicans." Spending far exceeded Revenues, the Debt was mammoth, and we were involved in a very unpopular war again. So it was an anti-Republican vote. And it happened. Obama swept into the White House and took a majority of Ds with him.

But, as often happens in the "off-year election" (a non-Presidential election), the tables were turned. Once again it was the recession that started in the waning months of the Bush second term. Predictably the Rs made great advancement in gaining control of the House (from down 257 to 178 to up 242 to 193), and by making the margin in the Senate even more non-veto proof (going from 57-41 to 51-47). In Iowa, the Rs won the Governor and the House, and moved to within two (24-26) in the Senate. It looks like 2012 will be very positive for the Rs as well. Here's why. (By the way, I did make these predictions publicly but not in a book.)

First of all, I don't believe the Recession was nearly as severe as we were told. "The worst since the Great Depression!" I heard this statement many times. Refer again to Schedule 3: Historical and Economic Data in the Appendix to help you understand this better.

Here are a few facts to compare the Recession of the late '70's through the early '80's to the one starting in 2008.

Unemployment reached 10.8% compared to 9.7%.
Inflation ramped up to 11.13% compared to less than 4%.
G.D.P. growth was the same at a depth of minus 0.2%.
The Prime Interest Rate reached 20% compared to less than 5%.
200+ banks closed annually compared to a range of 25 to 157.
Agriculture was terrible with many farm sales compared to favorable
    Ag. stats now.

The Auto Industry suffered greatly in both, but far more dealerships were lost in the '80's; however, there were more dealerships to begin with.

The Housing Industry was devastated in both, but for different reasons.

The Stock Markets crashed in the '70's/80's and has steadily increased in the first quarter of 2012.

The U.S. Dollar dipped significantly in both.

This Recession appears to be a bit longer than the earlier one, partially because the recovery is so tepid and slow.

Now evaluate, analyze, and make your own determination.

So what will happen in November, 2012? The economy is the key issue of course. Unemployment remains over 8% and goes down one month and up a little the next. The real reason it dropped at all is because more and more people got discouraged and dropped out of the labor force. Therefore, they are not even considered in the unemployment stats, even though they are not working. One has to be working, or collecting unemployment and applying for jobs to be included in the labor force. The true Unemployment Rate is well over 15%, and that doesn't count the under employed (those wanting to work more but can't). This, plus the fact that Obama's promise to reduce the debt and institute recovery hasn't happened or is occurring too slowly will cost him the Presidency. It will be just like 1980 when the anti-Carter vote put Ronald Reagan in the White House. Mitt Romney will be our next President. The House will stay with the Rs (even though a few seats will be lost) and the Senate will go to the Rs as well, but by a narrow margin. In Iowa, both the House and Senate will have a Republican majority. By the way, can you think of a President who has had a good or better second term?

Here is one of the main reasons why I think President Obama is in trouble. When elected he "hung his hat" on two main issues: "Obamacare" and "Cap in Trade" (this pertained to "keeping everything green"). Even his own party didn't like this last one, and it went nowhere. But "Obamacare" was passed, and it created much uncertainty in the business world. The business world hates uncertainty because it stagnates activity. Why does "Obamacare" create uncertainty? Because no one knows what it will cost, who will pay, how Medicare and Medicaid will be affected, or who has to pay for whose insurance, among other bothersome questions.

When Business doesn't know how much new employees will cost, they don't hire them. Hence unemployment remains a massive problem.

Maybe this analogy will help the understanding of how uncertainty freezes hiring, expansion, and additional risk taking. Let's say a woman finds a lump in her breast or a man discovers prostate problems (elevated PSA test). Biopsies are taken. Because the results aren't known for a period of time and there is uncertainty, no action is taken and much anxiety exists. Once the results are made known, whether they are positive or negative, action begins. I hope this explains the crippling effects of uncertainty. So that's the "last word."

We hope that you have a better understanding of how the Iowa legislature works, and we continue to encourage you to be involved. If you have questions or comments, we are always ready to visit. See our email addresses in the Appendix.

FRANK

Here are my thoughts on the outcomes for 2012.

I will take the road that the person who spends the most money in his/her election or reelection campaign will win. Statistics show that 98% of candidates who spend the most money get elected to office. Americans will see a record amount of money spent on the Presidential election, and I predict that President Obama will be re-elected to a second term. I will also predict that Iowans will see a record amount of money spent on the Senate race involving incumbent and majority leader Senator Mike Gronstal and his Republican opponent. I am hopeful that after this 2012 campaign, more states will begin to take steps in producing campaign finance legislation into law, including Iowa. This country doesn't need to have the person with the deepest pockets running the country, state, or county. It should be the best qualified person and one who will work hard to bring everyone to the table, listen to the concerns, and then provide the best leadership that they are able to.

I may disagree with some actions taken by our current and past legislators, but I can accept their decisions if they are based on hard facts and data as well as listening to the voices of the people. I am concerned about losing the middle class and creating an atmosphere of those who have it and those who don't.

Appendix

CHAPTER 1

ELASTIC AND INELASTIC DEMAND

Rule of Thumb: Needs/Necessities are **Price Inelastic**
Wants/Non-Necessities/Luxuries are **Price Elastic**

Price Elastic—A change in Price causes a bigger change in the Quantity Demanded.

Example: The Price of a 6-pack of pop goes down—so you buy two 6-packs instead of one.

Price Inelastic—A change in Price causes little or no change in Quantity Demanded

Example: The Price of a tube of toothpaste doubles—you still buy one tube.

A few business principles develop from knowledge of Price Elasticity. If the product is Price Elastic you drop the price as long as total revenue increases.

If the product is Price Inelastic (A necessity) don't drop the price because total revenue will decrease every time.

IOWA CIGARETTE TAX RECEIPTS FOR FY 2006-FY 2011

2006: $89,480,208
2007: $121,991,139
2008: $229,456,987

2009: $215,815,110
2010: $206,067,666
2011: $200,085,187

Note: On March 16, 2007, Iowa's cigarette tax rate increased from $0.36 to $1.36 per pack.

CHAPTER 2

ECCLESIASTES CHAPTER 10, VERSE 2 (NIV, 1983)

The heart of the wise inclines to the right, but the heart of the fool to the left.

RIGHT—LEFT—CENTER?

DIRECTIONS: Be sure to answer all questions and don't be afraid to indicate strong feelings. Indicate your feelings for each question by circling one of four responses. "SA" means you strongly agree and "A" indicates agreement with the statement. "D" is for disagreement and "SD" for strong disagreement. (Evaluation criteria follows this form.)

SA A D SD   1. I support a "laissez-faire" (hands-off or non-interference) philosophy regarding the Federal Government in the economy.

SA A D SD   2. Government should play a positive, activist role in stabilizing the economy during periodic episodes of inflation and/or unemployment.

SA A D SD   3. The competitive free-market system will allocate resources efficiently.

SA A D SD   4. Bureaucratic decision-making is inefficient, inhibiting, and mistake-ridden.

SA A D SD   5. I favor progress and reform in social institutions, individual freedom, and governmental guarantees of these rights and civil liberties.

SA A D SD   6. I believe in preserving what is established and resisting change.

SA A D SD   7. Fiscal policy (government spending and taxation) should be used to stabilize the economy.

SA A D SD   8. During times of high unemployment (7 to 10%) I favor a program of government-provided jobs in the public sector.

SA A D SD   9. The federal budget should be balanced and the national debt reduced.

SA A D SD   10. Minimum-wage laws, price supports, and pro-union legislation are desirable.

SA A D SD   11. I favor strong anti-monopoly laws.

SA A D SD   12. Waste in government is a major problem.

SA A D SD   13. Personal Income Tax reform, promoting equality in income and wealth distribution is imperative.

SA A D SD   14. Welfare, Aid to Families with Dependent Children, food stamps, and unemployment compensation programs must be maintained and possibly expanded.

SA A D SD   15. Competitive markets insure a just/fair distribution of income.

SA A D SD   16. I favor a strong United Nations.

SA A D SD   17. An increased percentage of the federal
                      budget should go to National Defense.

SA A D SD   18. The "welfare state" philosophy, of using
                      the government to protect society from
                      income loss, has gone too far.

SA A D SD   19. Federal spending, in relation to G.N.P.,
                      G.D.P. is too high.

SA A D SD   20. I favor legislation protecting our
                      environment, consumers, and the safety
                      of our workers.

SA A D SD   21. The USA should restrict imports in
                      order to reach a positive Balance of
                      Trade and benefit domestic labor.

SA A D SD   22. The government should leave things
                      like electric power and housing for
                      private business to handle.

SA A D SD   23. The Federal Government should
                      provide a National Health Care
                      program covering everyone.

SA A D SD   24. I don't favor gun control.

DIRECTIONS FOR EVALUATION: To find out if you are
Conservative, Moderate, or Liberal, this instrument guides you in
three ways.

FIRST: Circle the Numbers 2, 5, 7, 8, 10, 11, 13, 14, 16, 20,
              21, & 23. These statements are made with a Liberal
              slant. The others have a Conservative bent.

SECOND: Score the Liberal statements in the following way:
              SA = 4   A = 3   D = 2   SD = 1

Just write the scores next to the statement number.

THIRD: Now score the Conservative statements:
              SA = 1   A = 2   D = 3   SD = 4

FOURTH: Add up your score. The lower your score the more Conservative you are.

> Scores between 24 and 56 are Conservative
> 57 and 64 are Moderate
> 65 and 96 are Liberal

FIFTH: Count your number of strong feelings (4's and 1's). This will tell you which way you lean on the more important items to you.

SIXTH: Finally, see how many statements you scored like a Conservative (1's and 2's), and how many as a Liberal (3's and 4's). Of course if the majority are Conservative (13 or more), this also indicates what your preferences are.

Hopefully you see some consistency, but remember, you have a perfect right to be Conservative, Liberal, or Moderate. You don't have to defend yourself because our country needs all three! (Just for your own information, I have always scored in the Moderate range but am tending to get more Conservative as I get older. I don't know why!) I have administered this instrument over 10,000 times and the statements have been proven valid. By the way, #5 is the "book definition" of a Liberal and #6 defines Conservative.

CHAPTER 3

WHY THE NATIONAL DEBT DOESN'T HAVE TO BE PAID OFF!

The main reason is that the Federal Government doesn't die like we do. It doesn't have a final reckoning where a final settlement must be made. But it does have to be able to borrow (keep a positive credit rating). This means it has to pay off the notes and bonds when they become due (even if they have to borrow from someone else to do it). This means that most of the people and businesses that loan money to the Government can "live off the interest" and don't need the principal.

For example—if you have a million dollars loaned out and receive 5%—you can live off the $50,000 per year and don't need the million dollar principal back.

So how much is the United States worth? The internet gave the following information: the Federal Government owns 30% of all the land in the U.S., 4603 tons of gold (@ $1300 per ounce that amounts to nearly $600 Billion), the Federal Reserve has another $140 Billion in gold. The total value, when considering all of the buildings, highways, and other assets is about 116 Trillion Dollars. That means the Debt is about 11% of our country's value. Most banks will continue to loan money if your debt to capital ratio is 30 to 35%.

What are the dangers of the increasing national debt? The speed with which it rises. The selling off of assets. A decline in the value of land or other assets. Too much of the debt being loaned to foreign entities. United States people stop working and expect the Government to take care of us. BE PRODUCTIVE!

ECONOMIC FACT SHEET

The Discount Rate is 0.75%, the Fed. Funds Rate is 0.25%, the Prime Rate is 3.25%. The Fed. has a target of .25% and hasn't changed it for several years.

The National Debt is $15.7 T (May, 2012). It went up 1.2 T in '08; 1.89 T in '09; 1.65 T in '10; 1.23 T in '11; and 834 B so far in '12. Your individual share is now $50,064. How far can this go? (Population of the U.S. is 312 M.) (See www.usdebtclock.org for some amazing figures.)

In spite of what Clinton and some Congressmen say—there has not been a real surplus since '57.

Americans have continually imported more than we have exported since 1975!

12,800,000 shares were traded when the stock market crashed on Black Thursday in 1929. Typically, over 3 billion shares are traded daily now. Black Thursday was the start of the Great Depression.

Actual Interest paid on the National Debt was $230 B. in 2011. How can the Interest paid go down and the Debt keep rising? Look at the accurate figures on Table B-81.

The Unemployment Rate is 8.2%. It has been between 8% and 10% since 2008.

The Inflation Rate hasn't been over 4% since 1991. It was 3.8% for 2008; 0.35% in '09; 1.64% in '10; and 3.16% in '11. What will the trend be for the next few years?

Gold has risen significantly and stands at $1660. per troy ounce. What does that mean? Gold was $272.65 in 2000.

140 banks closed in 2009; 157 in '10; 92 in '11. What does this mean?

The average business sector worker makes $20.14 per hour. ($14.02 in 2002)

The U.S. Treas. owns 264 million troy ounces of gold. Based on $1660 per troy ounce, that's $438 B.

The Stock Market has been fluctuating and trending upward since 2008. The Dow Industrials were at 12,800 on Jan. 4, 2008, and 9035 at the start of '09. It closed at 13,228 at the end of April, 2012. What's your prediction for the close of 2012? Will the November elections make a difference?

* * *

What will the Prime Rate Do?

Why can the Federal Government continue to go deeper in debt and we can't?

How much has the National Debt risen in 2012? www.publicdebt.treas.gov

Has the Stock Market ever crashed as bad as it did on Black Thursday?

Is the dollar weaker or stronger? Which is better for you? www.x-rates.com

How serious is it if my bank goes under? How much does the FDIC insure deposits?

Are our American dollars backed up by gold and/or silver?

When will the Dow hit 14,000?

What countries use the Euro and what is it worth?

How much more would it take today to buy what $100 would buy the year you were born? www.bls.gov, then type in CPI Inflation Calculator.

Schedule 3 - Historical Economic Data

1 Year	2 Bank Failures	3 Civilian Unemployment Rate including resident armed forces	4 Prime Rate	5 CPI Inflation Rate	6 Real GDP Growth (1996 Dollars)	7 Growth of M1	8 Growth of M1
1920	168						
1921	505						
1922	367						
1923	646						
1924	775						
1925	618						
1926	976						
1927	669						
1928	499						
1929	659	3.20	5.50-6.00				
1930	1352	8.90					
1931	2294	16.30					
1932	1456	24.10					
1933	4004	25.20	1.50-4.00	(-0.51)			
1934	61	22.00	1.50				
1935	32	20.30	1.50				
1936	72	17.00	1.50				
1937	84	14.30	1.50				
1938	81	19.10	1.50				
1939	72	17.20	1.50	(-1.40)			
1940	48	14.60	1.50	0.7			
1941	17	9.90	1.50	5.0			
1942	23	4.70	1.50	10.90			
1943	5	1.90	1.50	6.10			
1944	2	1.20	1.50	1.70			
1945	1	1.90	1.50	2.30			
1946	2	3.90	1.50	8.30			
1947	6	3.90	1.52	14.40			
*1948	3	3.80	1.85	8.10			(-1.6)
*1949	9	5.90	2.00	(-1.20)			(-0.3)
1950	5	5.30	2.07	1.30			4.5
1951	5	3.30	2.56	7.90			5.6
1952	4	3.00	3.00	1.90			3.8
*1953	5	2.90	3.17	0.80			1.1
*1954	4	5.50	3.05	0.70			2.7
1955	5	4.40	3.16	(-.40)			2.2
1956	3	4.10	3.77	1.50			1.3
*1957	3	4.30	4.20	3.30			(-0.7)
*1958	9	6.80	3.83	2.80			3.8
1959	3	5.50	4.48	0.70	7.20		1.6
*1960	2	5.50	4.82	1.70	2.50	4.90	0.5
*1961	9	6.70	4.50	1.00	2.30	7.4	3.2
1962	3	5.50	4.50	1.00	6.00	8.1	1.8
1963	2	5.70	4.50	1.30	4.30	8.4	3.7
1964	8	5.20	4.50	1.30	5.80	8.0	4.6
1965	9	4.50	4.54	1.60	6.40	8.1	4.7
1966	8	3.80	5.63	2.90	6.60	4.6	2.5
1967	4	3.80	5.61	3.10	2.50	9.3	6.6
1968	3	3.60	6.30	4.20	4.80	-8.0	7.7
*1969	9	3.50	7.96	5.50	3.00	(-3.7)	3.3

1	2	3	4	5	6	7	8
Year	Bank Failures	Civilian Unemployment Rate including resident armed forces	Prime Rate	CPI Inflation Rate	GDP Growth (1996 Dollars)	Growth of M₂	Growth of M₁
*1970	8	4.90	7.91	5.70	.20	6.6	5.1
1971	6	5.90	5.72	4.40	3.30	13.4	6.5
1972	3	5.60	5.25	3.20	5.40	13.0	9.2
*1973	6	4.90	8.03	6.20	5.80	6.6	5.5
*1974	4	5.60	10.81	11.00	(-.60)	5.5	4.3
*1975	14	8.50	7.86	9.10	(-.40)	12.7	4.8
1976	17	7.70	6.84	5.80	5.60	13.3	6.6
1977	6	7.10	6.83	6.50	4.60	10.3	8.1
1978	7	6.10	9.06	7.60	5.50	7.6	8.2
1979	10	5.80	12.67	11.30	3.20	7.9	6.8
*1980	10	7.10	15.27	13.50	(-.20)	8.5	6.8
*1981	10	7.60	18.87	10.30	2.50	9.7	6.8
*1982	42	9.70	14.86	6.20	(-2.00)	8.8	8.7
1983	48	9.60	10.79	3.20	4.30	11.4	9.8
1984	79	7.50	12.04	4.30	7.30	8.7	5.9
1985	120	7.20	9.93	3.60	3.80	8.0	12.3
1986	138	7.00	8.33	1.90	3.40	9.5	16.9
1987	184	6.20	8.21	3.60	3.40	3.6	3.5
1988	200	5.50	9.32	4.10	4.20	5.8	5.0
1989	206	5.30	10.87	4.80	3.50	5.5	0.9
*1990	168	5.60	10.01	5.40	1.80	3.8	4.0
*1991	124	6.80	8.48	5.20	(-.50)	3.8	8.7
1992	120	7.50	6.25	3.00	3.00	1.6	14.3
1993	41	6.90	6.00	3.00	2.70	1.5	10.3
1994	4	6.10	7.15	2.60	4.00	0.4	1.8
1995	6	5.60	8.83	2.80	2.70	4.1	(-2.1)
1996	6	5.40	8.27	3.00	3.60	4.8	(-4.1)
1997	1	4.90	8.44	2.30	4.40	5.7	(-.7)
1998	3	4.50	8.35	1.56	4.30	8.8	2.2
1999	8	4.20	8.00	2.27	4.10	6.1	2.5
2000	7	4.00	9.23	3.37	3.7	6.1	(3.1)
* 2001	4	4.70	6.91	2.85	.8	10.5	8.7
2002	11	5.80	4.67	1.58	1.6	6.3	3.2
2003	3	6.00	4.12	2.27	2.5	5.0	7.1
2004	0	5.50	4.34	2.70	3.6	5.7	5.3
2005	0	5.10	6.19	3.40	3.1	4.1	-.1
2006	0	4.60	7.96	3.20	2.9	5.9	-.6
* 2007	3	4.60	8.05	2.80	3.8	6.0	.6
* 2008	25	5.80	5.09	3.80	2.6	10.0	16.8
* 2009	140	9.30	3.25	- .35	-2.5	3.4	5.7
* 2010	157	9.62	3.25	1.64	4.2	3.3	8.4
2011	92	8.95	3.25	3.16	3.9	9.6	18.1

* Recession Years
Sources: (FDIC) and the Economic Report of the President 2012

SCHEDULE 3: HISTORICAL AND ECONOMIC DATA

TABLE B-81. Federal receipts, outlays, surplus or deficit, and debt, fiscal years 2006–2011

[Millions of dollars; fiscal years]

Description	Actual 2006	Actual 2007	Actual 2008	Actual 2009	Estimates 2010	Estimates 2011
RECEIPTS, OUTLAYS, AND SURPLUS OR DEFICIT						
Total:						
Receipts	2,406,876	2,568,001	2,523,999	2,104,995	2,165,119	2,567,181
Outlays	2,655,057	2,728,702	2,982,554	3,517,681	3,720,701	3,833,861
Surplus or deficit (–)	–248,181	–160,701	–458,555	–1,412,686	–1,555,582	–1,266,680
On-budget:						
Receipts	1,798,494	1,932,912	1,865,953	1,450,986	1,529,936	1,893,113
Outlays	2,232,988	2,275,065	2,507,803	3,000,665	3,163,742	3,255,668
Surplus or deficit (–)	–434,494	–342,153	–641,850	–1,549,679	–1,633,806	–1,362,555
Off-budget:						
Receipts	608,382	635,089	658,046	654,009	635,183	674,068
Outlays	422,069	453,637	474,751	517,016	556,959	578,193
Surplus or deficit (–)	186,313	181,452	183,295	136,993	78,224	95,875
OUTSTANDING DEBT, END OF PERIOD						
Gross Federal debt	8,451,350	8,950,744	9,986,082	11,875,851	13,786,615	15,144,029
Held by Federal Government accounts	3,622,378	3,915,615	4,183,032	4,331,144	4,488,962	4,645,704
Held by the public	4,829,972	5,035,129	5,803,050	7,544,707	9,297,653	10,498,325
Federal Reserve System	768,924	779,632	491,127	769,160	....	....
Other	4,060,048	4,255,497	5,311,923	6,775,547	....	....
RECEIPTS BY SOURCE						
Total: On-budget and off-budget	2,406,876	2,568,001	2,523,999	2,104,995	2,165,119	2,567,181
Individual income taxes	1,043,908	1,163,472	1,145,747	915,308	935,771	1,121,296
Corporation income taxes	353,915	370,243	304,346	138,229	156,741	296,902
Social insurance and retirement receipts	837,821	869,607	900,155	890,917	875,756	935,116
On-budget	229,439	234,518	242,109	236,908	240,573	261,048
Off-budget	608,382	635,089	658,046	654,009	635,183	674,068
Excise taxes	73,981	65,069	67,334	62,483	73,204	74,288
Estate and gift taxes	27,877	26,044	28,844	23,482	17,011	25,035
Customs duties and fees	24,810	26,010	27,568	22,453	23,787	27,445
Miscellaneous receipts	44,584	47,556	50,005	52,123	82,849	87,099
Deposits of earnings by Federal Reserve System	29,945	32,043	33,598	34,318	77,083	79,341
Allowances [1]	....	....	....	....	–12,000	–9,000
All other	14,639	15,513	16,407	17,805	17,766	16,758
OUTLAYS BY FUNCTION						
Total: On-budget and off-budget	2,655,057	2,728,702	2,982,554	3,517,681	3,720,701	3,833,861
National defense	521,827	551,271	616,073	661,049	719,179	749,748
International affairs	29,499	28,482	28,857	37,529	51,138	54,192
General science, space and technology	23,584	25,525	27,731	29,449	33,032	31,554
Energy	782	–860	628	4,749	18,952	24,863
Natural resources and environment	33,028	31,732	31,825	35,574	47,039	42,537
Agriculture	25,969	17,662	18,387	22,237	26,610	25,590
Commerce and housing credit	6,187	487	27,870	291,535	–25,319	22,127
On-budget	7,262	–4,606	25,453	291,231	–31,745	17,901
Off-budget	–1,075	5,093	2,417	304	6,426	4,226
Transportation	70,244	72,905	77,616	84,289	106,458	104,189
Community and regional development	54,465	29,567	23,952	27,650	28,469	31,973
Education, training, employment, and social services	118,482	91,656	91,287	79,746	142,521	128,399
Health	252,739	266,382	280,599	334,327	372,336	400,661
Medicare	329,868	375,407	390,758	430,093	457,159	497,341
Income security	352,477	365,975	431,313	533,224	685,870	595,005
Social security	548,549	586,153	617,027	682,963	721,496	736,284
On-budget	16,058	19,307	17,830	34,071	37,629	27,664
Off-budget	532,491	566,846	599,197	648,892	683,867	708,620
Veterans benefits and services	69,811	72,818	84,653	95,429	124,655	124,539
Administration of justice	41,016	41,244	47,138	51,549	55,025	57,280
General government	18,177	17,425	20,325	22,026	29,290	27,670
Net interest	226,603	237,109	252,757	186,902	187,772	250,709
On-budget	324,325	343,112	366,475	304,856	306,176	369,789
Off-budget	–97,722	–106,003	–113,718	–117,954	–118,404	–119,080
Allowances					18,750	21,676
Undistributed offsetting receipts	–68,250	–82,238	–86,242	–92,639	–79,731	–90,476
On-budget	–56,625	–69,939	–73,097	–78,413	–64,801	–74,903
Off-budget	–11,625	–12,299	–13,145	–14,226	–14,930	–15,573

[1] Includes Allowances for Health Reform and the Jobs Bill.

Note: See Note, Table B-78.

Sources: Department of the Treasury and Office of Management and Budget.

Appendix B

TABLE B-81: *Federal receipts, outlays, surplus or deficit, and debt, fiscal years 2008-2013*

TABLE B–89. Estimated ownership of U.S. Treasury securities, 1998–2011

[Billions of dollars]

End of month	Total public debt[1]	Federal Reserve and Intragovernmental holdings[2]	Total privately held	Depository institutions[3]	U.S. savings bonds[4]	Pension funds: Private[5]	Pension funds: State and local governments	Insurance companies	Mutual funds[6]	State and local governments	Foreign and international[7]	Other investors[8]	% owed to foreigners
1998 Mar	5,542.4	2,104.9	3,437.5	308.3	181.2	141.3	212.1	169.5	234.6	238.1	1,250.5	701.9	
June	5,547.9	2,198.6	3,349.3	280.9	180.7	139.0	213.2	160.6	230.0	255.5	1,256.0	619.8	22.8%
Sept	5,526.2	2,213.0	3,313.2	244.5	180.8	135.5	207.8	151.4	231.7	771.8	1,224.2	685.4	
Dec	5,614.2	2,280.2	3,334.0	227.4	180.3	133.7	212.6	141.7	257.6	280.8	1,278.7	611.7	
1999 Mar	5,651.6	2,324.1	3,327.5	247.4	180.6	135.5	211.5	137.5	245.0	288.4	1,272.3	609.4	22.9%
June	5,638.8	2,438.6	3,199.2	240.6	180.0	142.9	213.8	133.6	226.1	288.6	1,256.8	502.7	
Sept	5,656.3	2,480.9	3,175.4	241.2	180.0	150.3	204.8	128.0	222.5	293.2	1,291.4	467.3	
Dec	5,776.1	2,542.2	3,233.8	248.7	179.3	153.0	180.8	173.4	228.7	304.5	1,266.7	526.0	
2000 Mar	5,773.4	2,590.6	3,182.8	237.7	176.6	150.2	196.9	120.0	222.3	306.3	1,085.0	685.7	18.3%
June	5,685.9	2,698.6	2,987.3	222.2	177.7	149.0	194.9	116.5	205.4	309.3	1,060.7	551.7	
Sept	5,674.2	2,737.9	2,936.3	220.5	177.7	147.9	185.5	113.7	207.8	307.9	1,038.8	536.5	
Dec	5,662.2	2,781.8	2,880.4	201.5	176.9	145.0	179.1	110.2	225.7	310.0	1,015.2	516.9	
2001 Mar	5,773.7	2,880.9	2,892.8	180.0	184.8	153.4	177.3	108.1	225.3	318.9	1,012.5	525.4	17.7%
June	5,726.8	3,004.2	2,722.6	168.1	185.5	148.5	163.1	108.1	221.6	324.8	983.3	380.2	
Sept	5,807.5	3,027.8	2,779.7	185.1	186.5	149.3	156.8	106.8	234.1	321.2	992.2	433.1	
Dec	5,943.4	3,123.9	2,819.5	181.5	190.4	145.8	155.1	105.7	261.9	328.4	1,040.1	410.5	
2002 Mar	6,006.0	3,156.8	2,849.2	187.6	192.0	152.7	163.3	114.0	266.1	327.8	1,057.2	388.8	19.5%
June	6,126.5	3,276.7	2,849.8	204.7	192.8	152.1	153.9	122.0	253.8	333.6	1,135.4	313.7	
Sept	6,228.2	3,303.5	2,924.8	209.3	193.3	154.5	156.3	130.4	258.8	338.6	1,180.6	298.9	
Dec	6,405.7	3,387.2	3,018.5	222.6	194.9	153.8	150.9	139.7	281.0	354.7	1,235.6	277.4	
2003 Mar	6,460.8	3,390.8	3,070.0	153.6	196.9	165.8	162.1	139.5	296.6	350.0	1,275.2	330.2	21.9%
June	6,670.1	3,505.4	3,164.7	145.4	199.2	170.2	161.3	138.7	302.3	347.0	1,371.9	327.6	
Sept	6,783.2	3,515.3	3,267.9	146.8	201.6	197.7	155.5	137.4	287.1	357.7	1,443.3	371.0	
Dec	6,998.0	3,620.1	3,377.9	163.1	203.9	172.2	142.6	138.5	280.9	364.2	1,523.1	395.4	
2004 Mar	7,131.1	3,628.3	3,502.8	162.0	204.5	189.8	143.6	172.4	280.8	374.1	1,670.0	324.8	24.1%
June	7,274.3	3,742.8	3,531.5	158.6	204.6	173.3	134.9	174.8	258.7	381.2	1,735.4	310.1	
Sept	7,378.1	3,772.0	3,607.1	138.5	204.2	174.0	140.8	182.9	255.0	381.7	1,794.5	335.5	
Dec	7,596.1	3,905.6	3,690.5	125.0	204.5	173.7	151.0	188.5	254.1	389.1	1,849.3	355.4	
2005 Mar	7,776.9	3,921.6	3,855.3	141.8	204.2	177.3	158.0	193.3	261.1	412.0	1,952.2	355.5	24.9%
June	7,836.5	4,033.5	3,803.0	128.9	204.2	181.0	171.3	195.0	248.7	444.0	1,877.5	354.4	
Sept	7,932.7	4,067.8	3,864.9	125.3	203.6	184.2	184.8	200.7	244.7	467.6	1,929.5	344.3	
Dec	8,170.4	4,199.8	3,970.6	117.1	205.2	184.9	153.8	202.3	251.3	481.4	2,033.9	340.6	
2006 Mar	8,371.2	4,257.2	4,114.0	113.0	206.0	186.7	153.0	200.3	246.7	473.3	2,082.1	450.8	24.3%
June	8,420.0	4,389.2	4,030.8	119.5	205.2	192.1	150.9	196.1	244.2	484.2	1,894.7	460.8	
Sept	8,507.0	4,432.8	4,074.2	113.6	203.7	201.5	154.7	195.8	235.7	494.9	2,025.3	457.5	
Dec	8,680.2	4,558.1	4,122.1	114.8	202.4	207.5	156.2	197.9	250.7	506.8	2,103.1	382.7	
2007 Mar	8,849.7	4,576.6	4,273.1	119.8	200.3	221.7	150.3	185.4	264.5	548.2	2,194.8	382.0	24.8%
June	8,867.7	4,715.1	4,152.6	110.4	198.6	232.5	159.3	168.9	267.7	560.3	2,192.0	753.7	
Sept	9,007.7	4,738.0	4,269.7	119.7	197.1	246.7	138.9	155.1	306.3	526.8	2,235.3	343.7	
Dec	9,229.2	4,833.5	4,395.7	179.8	196.5	257.8	141.6	141.9	362.9	525.1	2,353.2	287.2	
2008 Mar	9,437.6	4,694.7	4,742.9	125.0	195.4	270.5	142.0	152.1	484.4	524.9	2,506.3	342.2	28.0%
June	9,492.0	4,696.0	4,906.7	112.7	195.0	276.7	141.8	159.4	472.2	513.4	2,587.4	342.5	
Sept	10,024.7	4,692.7	5,332.0	130.0	194.3	332.5	143.9	163.4	656.1	493.9	2,802.4	455.5	
Dec	10,699.8	4,806.4	5,893.4	105.0	194.1	297.2	146.4	171.4	788.8	475.1	3,077.2	658.3	
2009 Mar	11,126.9	4,785.2	6,341.7	125.6	194.0	330.9	150.2	191.0	715.9	508.0	3,265.7	860.4	29.5%
June	11,545.3	5,026.8	6,518.5	140.8	193.6	353.4	158.9	200.0	695.6	504.7	3,460.6	803.7	
Sept	11,909.8	5,127.1	6,782.7	198.1	192.5	398.1	167.3	210.2	644.9	492.3	3,570.8	908.7	
Dec	12,311.3	5,276.9	7,034.4	207.4	191.3	479.8	174.5	222.0	666.2	493.9	3,685.1	969.1	
2010 Mar	12,773.1	5,259.8	7,513.3	269.4	190.3	462.2	179.1	225.7	646.4	499.9	3,877.9	1,162.5	31.6%
June	13,201.8	5,345.1	7,856.7	266.1	189.7	531.9	182.0	231.8	632.1	504.8	4,070.0	1,248.4	
Sept	13,561.6	5,350.5	8,211.1	372.9	188.8	590.5	185.5	240.6	607.4	498.1	4,324.2	1,248.5	
Dec	14,025.2	5,056.2	6,360.5	319.1	188.0	615.9	185.6	248.4	637.9	503.6	4,435.5	1,234.9	
2011 Mar	14,270.0	5,958.9	8,311.1	321.2	186.0	632.9	187.9	246.9	641.1	486.8	4,473.6	1,123.8	31.6%
June	14,343.1	6,220.4	8,122.7	279.3	186.1	650.7	186.9	246.1	653.1	479.3	4,511.1	922.1	
Sept	14,790.3	6,328.0	8,462.4	292.2	185.2	689.6	186.7	253.7	698.0	460.8	4,667.0	1,026.2	
Dec	15,222.8		9,439.6	1,783.2	185.3								

(Handwritten note across bottom of columns: 42.3% | 59.7% | 1.8% | 4.7% | 1.3% | 1.7% | 9.7% | 3.1% | 31.6% | 6.9%)

[1] Face value.
[2] Federal Reserve holdings exclude Treasury securities held under repurchase agreements.
[3] Includes commercial banks, savings institutions, and credit unions.
[4] Current accrual value.
[5] Includes Treasury securities held by the Federal Employees Retirement System Thrift Savings Plan "G Fund."
[6] Includes money market mutual funds, mutual funds, and closed-end investment companies.
[7] Includes nonmarketable foreign series, Treasury securities, and Treasury deposit funds. Excludes Treasury securities held under repurchase agreements in custody accounts at the Federal Reserve Bank of New York. Estimates reflect benchmarks in this series at differing intervals; for further detail, see Treasury Bulletin at http://www.treas.gov/tic/ticsec2.shtml.
[8] Includes individuals, Government-sponsored enterprises, brokers and dealers, bank personal trusts and estates, corporate and noncorporate businesses, and other investors.

Note: Data shown in this table are as of January 20, 2012.
Source: Department of the Treasury.

TABLE B-89: *Estimated ownership of U.S. Treasury securities, 1998-2011*

The numbers written across the bottom are my calculations of what percent of the national debt is borrowed from the entities listed across the top of the table.

The percents beside the right-hand column are what percent of the national debt is borrowed from foreign countries. Notice that we are borrowing more than we need.

CORNERSTONES OF CAPITALISM

1. Private Property
2. Free Enterprise
3. Free Markets
4. Profit Motive
5. Competition

LEADING ECONOMIC INDICATORS

1. Unemployment Rate
2. Weekly Earnings
3. Gross Domestic Product
4. Inventories
5. Durable Goods Orders
6. Personal Income
7. Consumer Price Index
8. Producer Price Index
9. New Construction
10 New Housing Permits
11. International Trade Balance

CHAPTER 5

In 1932, Adolph Hitler said, "The streets of our country are in turmoil. The universities are filled with students rebelling and rioting. Communists are seeking to destroy our country. Russia is threatening us with her might, and the Republic is in danger. Yes, danger from within and without. We need law and order. Yes, without law and order, our nation cannot survive. Elect us and we shall restore law and order."

CHAPTER 9

Number of Terms Served by Members of Iowa's 83rd General Assembly 2009-10

SENATE			*HOUSE*	
Number of Terms	Number of Members		Number of Terms	Number of Members
1	9		1	18
2	19		2	13
3	11		3	11
4	4		4	24
5	3		5	8
7	2		6	10
8	2		7	5
			8	5
			9	3
			11	2
			12	1

Of the 18 House members who did not run or were defeated, 3 members were in their 1st term, 1 in 2nd, 5 in 3rd, 2 in 5th, 1 in 6th, 3 in 7th, and 1 in each of their 8th, 9th, and 11th.

Of the 7 Senators who retired, 1 was in his 1st, (Guess Who!), 2 in 2nd, 3 in 3rd, and 1 in 5th.
Of the two incumbents who were defeated, one was in his 1st, and the other in his 3rd.
The Speaker of the House is in his 11th term. The previous speaker is in his 9th.
The Senate Majority Leader is in his 7th.

NUMBER OF TERMS OF MEMBERS OF IOWA'S 83RD GENERAL ASSEMBY 2009-10

STATE	POPULATION (In millions)	SENATORS	REPS	SESSION LENGTH (Days)
1. Alabama	4.6	35	105	103
2. Alaska	683 T.	20	40	90
3. *Arizona*	6.3	30	60	85
4. *Arkansas*	2.8	35	100	112 **
5. *California*	36.5	40	80	275
6. *Colorado*	4.8	35	65	120
7. Connecticut	3.5	36	151	92
8. Delaware	864 T.	21	41	174
9. *Florida*	18.2	40	120	59
10. Georgia	9.5	56	180	94
11. Hawaii	1.2	25	51	112
12. Idaho	1.5	35	70	90
13. Illinois	12.8	59	118	360
14. Indiana	6.3	50	100	114
15. Iowa	3.0	50	100	110
16. Kansas	2.7	40	125	106
17. Kentucky	4.2	38	100	83
18. *Louisiana*	4.3	39	105	85
19. *Maine*	1.3	35	151	104
20. Maryland	5.6	46	141	88
21. Massachusetts	6.4	40	160	360
22. *Michigan*	10.0	38	110	360
23. Minnesota	5.2	67	134	96
24. *Missouri*	5.8	34	163	127
25. Mississippi	2.9	52	122	124
26. *Montana*	957 T.	50	100	90 **
27. *Nebraska*	1.7	49 in Unicameral		96
28. *Nevada*	2.5	21	42	118 **
29. New Hampshire	1.3	24	400	179
30. New Jersey	8.7	40	80	360
31. New Mexico	1.9	42	70	30
32. New York	19.3	62	150	360
33. North Carolina	9.0	50	120	74
34. North Dakota	639 T.	47	94	110 **
35. *Ohio*	11.4	33	99	360
36. *Oklahoma*	3.6	48	101	115
37. Oregon	3.7	30	60	172 **
38. Pennsylvania	12.4	50	203	330
39. Rhode Island	1.0	38	75	181
40. South Carolina	4.4	46	124	148
41. *South Dakota*	796 T.	35	70	68
42. Tennessee	6.1	33	99	135
43. Texas	23.9	31	150	139 **
44. Utah	2.6	29	75	49
45. Vermont	621 T.	30	150	143
46. Virginia	7.7	40	100	68
47. Washington	6.4	49	98	58
48. West Virginia	1.8	34	100	58
49. Wisconsin	5.6	33	99	350
50. Wyoming	520 T.	30	60	24

** These states meet Every Other Year. Most also have a short (less than a month) Session in the "off" year. 18 States have more Legislators than Iowa and 21 meet for longer sessions.

36 states have Term Limits for Governors. The 14 that DON'T are UNDERLINED.

15 states have Term Limits for Legislators. They are in **Bold Print and Italics**.

Note: None of the states that have Term Limits have them for both the Governor and Legislators. Why is that, do you suppose?

LEGISLATIVE INFORMATION FOR ALL STATES

IOWA LEGISLATURE

Gen. Assembly	Years	Governor	Senate # R	Senate # D	House # R	House # D	Political Party Gov	Political Party S	Political Party H
63rd	1969-70	Ray	45	16	86	38	R	R	R
64th	71-72	Ray	37	13	63	37	R	R	R
65th	73-74	Ray	28	22	55	45	R	R	R
66th	75-76	Ray	24	26	34	61	R	D	D
67th	77-78	Ray	24	26	41	59	R	D	D
68th	79-80	Ray	28	22	56	44	R	R	R
69th	81-82	Ray	29	21	58	42	R	R	R
70th	83-84	Branstad	22	28	40	60	R	D	D
71st	85-86	Branstad	21	29	40	60	R	D	D
72nd	87-88	Branstad	20	30	42	58	R	D	D
73rd	89-90	Branstad	20	30	39	61	R	D	D
74th	91-92	Branstad	22	28	45	55	R	D	D
75th	93-94	Branstad	23	27	51	49	R	D	R
76th	95-96	Branstad	23	27	64	36	R	D	R
77th	97-98	Branstad	28	22	54	46	R	R	R
78th	99-00	Vilsack	30	20	56	44	D	R	R
79th	2001-02	Vilsack	30	20	56	44	D	R	R
80th	03-04	Vilsack	29	21	54	46	D	R	R
81st	05-06	Vilsack	25	25	51	49	D	=	R
82nd	07-08	Culver	20	30	46	54	D	D	D
83rd	09-10	Culver	18	32	44	56	D	D	D
84th	11-12	Branstad	24	26	60	40	R	D	R

Quick Summary   Governor Ray – Republicans in complete control 5 General Assemblies
Senate and House Controlled by Democrats 2 Gen. Asmb.

Governor Branstad – R's in complete control for 1 Gen. Assembly
D's in complete control for 5 Gen. Assemblies
House by R's and Senate by D's for 2 Gen. Assem.

Governor Vilsack – R's in complete control for 3 Gen. Assemblies
Senate equal and House by R's for 1 Gen. Assembly

Governor Culver – D's in complete control for 2 General Assemblies

Governor Branstad – House R's and Senate D's for 1 General Assembly

One Party in Complete Control 8 of 22   (6 by R's and 2 by D's)
Governor Controls 1 Party with the House and Senate from the opposite Party 10 of 22 (7 D's and 3 R's)

Governor and the House controlled by one Party – 3 of 22 (All by R's)

Governor from one Party, House from the other, and the Senate tied – 1 of 22

IOWA LEGISLATURE 1969-PRESENT

Term Limits Lessons for Campaign Reform

by Patrick Basham

Patrick Basham is senior fellow in the Center for Representative Government at the Cato Institute.

Added to *cato.org* on August 31, 2001

This article appeared on cato.org *on August 31, 2001.*

Eleven years after the first successful initiative, term limits have affected more than 700 legislative seats in 11 states. At a time of anticipation over the reform of our campaign system, the term limits experiment has much to tell us.

Lesson One. Term limits stimulate political competition. That is accomplished in a variety of ways, from increasing the number of open seats and special elections to lowering the reelection rates of incumbents. Many former incumbents return to private life, and a significant number run for other offices, thereby stimulating political competition at other levels. There is also evidence to suggest that campaigns may be less costly in a term-limited electoral environment. Under term limits, California's state campaign spending since 1992 is 44 percent lower than from 1984 to 1988.

Lesson Two. Term limits increase legislative diversity. The prospect of shorter political careers is also changing the characteristics of people who choose to seek public office, encouraging political participation by nonprofessional politicians. Hence, the occupational makeup of state legislatures is gradually moving away from the traditional preponderance of ex-lawyers and ex-political aides. In California in 1995 there were only 3.4 percent self-described full-time state legislators, down from 36 percent in 1986, and three times more legislators are now business people than were previously.

Making the legislature closer to the private sector also familiarizes legislators with the complex consequences of laws and regulations. Overall, a state legislature composed of average citizens is a legislature that looks more like America (California?) and less like a political class of arrogant and ambitious politicians intent on self-aggrandizement.

Greater occupational diversity is paralleled by greater gender and racial diversity. As predicted by proponents, the number of successful female and minority candidates has risen. Female candidates seem to find it easier to gain entry to term-limited legislatures than to non-term-limited legislatures and are more likely to gain leadership positions in high-turnover legislatures. The same is true for minority candidates. A recent survey of the term-limited Michigan legislature found a 42 percent increase in female state House members and a 65 percent increase in African-American state House members.

Lesson Three. Term-limited legislatures undergo positive institutional changes. As institutions, they become more merit based and less governed by an outdated seniority system. Term limits eliminate the possibility of entrenched legislative leaders dominating a legislative chamber. Leadership positions (especially that of Speaker) become less powerful as a more decentralized power structure evolves in response to the growing independence of term-limited freshmen legislators. Generally speaking, freshman legislators tend to ask tougher questions of bureaucrats and demand a higher level of performance from government agencies than did their predecessors.

Has the alleged loss of knowledge and experience dealt a devastating blow to the term-limited state legislatures? The evidence accumulated to date suggests that the fears of critics are unwarranted. In many instances, the loss of institutional memory, legislative knowledge, and political experience has fostered a more energetic, more ideological, and more effective deliberative body. There is little evidence to suggest that (contrary to the predictions of critics of term limits) the bureaucracy, the interest group lobbyists, or the legislative staffs have filled the "experience void" to the detriment of state-level democracy or public policy.

Lesson Four. Term limits act as a natural campaign finance reform. Term limits diminish the value of a legislative seat to lobbyists and the special interests they represent in state capitals. That reduces the incentive for lobbyists to raise and to distribute the large "soft money" contributions so disliked by the political establishment. In states as dissimilar as Maine, Michigan, and Ohio there is evidence that lobbyists are unsettled by the term limits-induced need to build new political relationships from scratch.

Lesson Five. Term limits improve the quality of legislation. The continual infusion of fresh blood into state legislatures is improving public policy. By mandating frequent legislative turnover, term limits are bringing new perspectives to state legislatures, reducing the concentration on reelection, and thereby diminishing the incentive for wasteful election-related pork barrel spending that flourishes in a careerist legislative culture.

There are clear indications that term limits foster institutional settings that are favorable to smaller government. Studies show that the longer an individual stays in office, the greater his support for increased government spending. Limiting terms may lead to limited government, or at least a smaller government than would have existed in their absence. A pattern is developing across the term-limited states. In Arizona, California, Colorado, Florida, Maine, Montana, and Ohio, the composition of the legislature is evolving from higher spending professional legislators to more fiscally conservative citizen legislators.

In 1990, Oklahoma became the first state to term limit its legislators. Eleven years later a majority of term-limited states are experiencing campaigns to repeal those laws. Nonetheless, the evidence says we should be extending, rather than ending, the term limits experiment.

PATRICK BASHAM: TERM LIMITS LESSONS FOR CAMPAIGN REFORM

CHAPTER 10

SPECIAL PEOPLE AT THE CAPITOL

All these have our heartfelt admiration and respect.

Computer Specialists: Val Van Vlair Hansen and Joe Kroes

Senate Doorkeepers: Jerry Carlson, Jim Douglas, Bob Langbehn, Frank Loeffel, Kerm Tannatt, Bob White, and Sergeant-at-Arms Bill Kreig, Assistant Sgt. Tom Sheldahl.

Indispensable Servants (friends) in the Senate: Mike Marshall (Secretary of the Senate), K'Ann Brandt (Confidential Secretary to Secretary of the Senate), Cindy Clingan (Sr. Assistant Secretary of the Senate), Betty Shea (Administrative Secretary to Secretary of the Senate), Lois Brownell and Linda Laurenzo (Sr. Finance Officers), Janet Hawkins, Maureen Lee Taylor, and Angela Cox (Journal Editors), Kathleen Curoe (Indexer/Records and Supply), Kathy Olah (Sr. Indexer), Jay Mosher (Bill Clerk), Jo Ann Larson and Sue Ellen Hudson, ("The Telephone Ladies"), Leila Carlson (Postmistress).

Republican Caucus Staff: Kirsten Anderson, Tom Ashworth, Pam Dugdale, Jim Friedrich, Carolann Jensen, Angie Lewis, Peter Matthes (Director), Russ Trimble, Carol Wieck, Brent Oleson. Democrat Caucus Staff: Eric Bakker, Kris Bell, Steve Conway, Catherine Engel, Bridget Godes, Kassie Hobbs, Debbie Kattenhorn, Theresa Kehoe, Kay Kibbe, Rusty Martin, Jace Mikels, Sue Monahan, Kellee Mullen, Ron Parker (Director), Erica Shorkey, Julie Simon, Kerry Wright.

CHAPTER 11 THE FINALE

LAWS THAT NEED ATTENTION

1. Federal Government: Change the law that makes every child born in the U.S. a citizen when neither parent is a resident or citizen.
2. Institute 12-year Term Limits on newly elected Iowa legislators.
3. Change Senate term to 6 years in Iowa. Change House term to 4 years in Iowa.
4. Legalize Fireworks in Iowa (I hate laws that aren't enforced)
5. We have to do something positive about illegal immigrants, especially kids that have lived most of their lives in the U.S., have been educated in our schools, are good citizens, and now want to go on to college or get the jobs they want. Maybe finding sponsors (possibly the employers) for all illegals presently here and working. This is a ***tough*** one but something has to be done.
6. Disallow the use of the word *"Notwithstanding"* in all Bills and Amendments. Basically this word supersedes any action that has been previously passed. By inserting "notwithstanding" into any phrase it makes absolutely no difference as to what has been passed before. We should all be very suspicious of the law and any person who insists on its usage.
7. Get another penny for the Bottle and Can Redemption Centers. Don't go to curbside recycling.
8. Questions to Consider: Does a state with a population of 3 million need 150 Legislators? Do we need 99 counties and all the offices duplicated in each regardless of population? Do we need two High School Athletic Associations?
9. Sales Tax on all internet sales is vital. Rationale—More and more people are purchasing items on line and paying no sales tax. This internet competition is taking a lot of business away from our local commercial businesses and reducing our state

revenues which will necessitate hikes in other taxes or fees. Think about it.

EMAILS

Frank Wood: frank.wood@north-scott.k12.ia.us
Dave Mulder: wplusd@mtcnet.net

About the Authors

Frank B. Wood, Jr. Married 39 years to Peggy, with two children: Brian and Lindsey, and five grandchildren. Has worked 39 years in public education in three different school systems in Illinois and Iowa as a teacher, coach, and administrator. Served one term as Mayor of Eldridge, Iowa. Served one term as Iowa State Senator.

Dave Mulder, born in Alton Iowa, 1939. Married 50 years to Dot with two children: Dick and Amy, and two grandchildren (Sarah and Ethan). He is a lifelong educator and coach—20 years in Sioux Center Community Schools and 25 years at Northwestern College. Published *Devotions from the Heartland* in 2010. Served one term as Iowa State Senator.

Contact Info:

Frank B. Wood, Jr.
1135 W. Davies Street
Eldridge, Iowa 52748 email: frank.wood@north-scott.k12.ia.us

Dave Mulder
1452 3rd Ave. NE
Sioux Center, Iowa 51250 email: wplusd@mtcnet.net